Motives in Your Life

Understanding and Applying Personal Motives

Chris Brown
God Bless you

Motives in Your Life

Understanding and Applying Personal Motives

Thomas A Browdy
Alberts Adams Institute
Saint Louis, Missouri

albertsadamsllc@gmail.com

This publication is designed to be used for personal preferences discovery. This book is not provided to recommend professional opinion nor guarantee results.

Browdy, Thomas A.
© 2024 by Thomas A. Browdy.

ISBN 978-0-9825362-3-0

To my darling wife Karen

Acknowledgements
It is a pleasure to remember those who have
contributed to this work. John Shaffer who opened
his mind to this area of interest and reviewed all the
content and contributed to the scoring format. Mike
McDermid for his years of scoring stories with me.
Plus, those who have contributed thoughts and
suggestions: Colleagues Richard Diehl, Hudson
Guthrie, Larry Pionke, John Bechtoldt, and John
Williamson. My appreciation goes to Ingrid Anderson
Florman and her excellent editing skills. And finally,
to students and alumni in the Washington
University's graduate programs in Information
Management, Engineering Management, and Project
Management – ever challenging and pushing
boundaries of interest.

Preface

Understanding Motives

Motives are key to what we do. When asked about our motives we respond with something that we think reflects our motives. These are our conscious or cognitive motives, what we espouse as our motives. Yet one's behavior frequently seems at odds with our espoused motives. Why? The reason is that people have natural motives, baked into our personality over years of experiences, which override what we say; natural motives reflect what we have an actual tendency to do. And natural motives are sometimes at odds with motives we state. Why? Natural motives are there but are frequently obscured by the current situation and one's desire to "look good."

This book was written to provide information about natural human motives that have been mostly ignored. The book focuses on the motives that come natural for people. The four key motives of *achievement, affiliation, power,* and *personal causation* are explained and examined in detail. These four motives, alone and in combination, have been found to be the foundation of personalities and how we respond to situations.

The need to discover and apply personal motives was revealed while teaching classes on leadership over a period of fifteen years. I found that people in the classes did not understand what sort of leadership character would be natural for them. There are certain ways to lead that one person would find more natural than another. After performing an analysis of motives, it was possible for class participants to understand a pathway they could follow toward more effective leadership in their careers. They often ask questions about how their motive analysis could improve other parts of their lives. It became obvious that natural motives were a leading indicator of job satisfaction. In the accompanying motives workbook motives are connected with various job and professional positions. Since motives are learned, any job can potentially be a good fit provided your present motives, or motives that you could learn, fit the job. The key is to know your natural motives.

When motives were combined into what were called syndromes, the application of motives to other circumstances in life became evident. A motive syndrome is a combination of two, or more predominant motives from the four key motives. Using motive syndromes, it is possible to understand individual personalities, as well as personal preferences such as, how people make decisions, and the kinds of groups they would find attractive.

Motives are fairly stable over time, but with the appropriate kind of training motives can be changed. It is important to find out which motives would be most valuable to change given a person's expectations and situation. This book can reveal not only your motives, but which motives might be most beneficial to change, and how to change them.

Another reason for this book is to bring back awareness of the importance of projective testing as found in the Thematic Apperception Test (TAT). This test has been essentially ignored for many years primarily because it requires human intelligence to score. Therefore, it is more time consuming than a simple question rating or ranking test that can be scored by a computer.

The TAT is a projective psychological test developed during the 1930s by Henry Murray and Christiana Morgan at Harvard University. Murray, a devotee to Herman Melville, was looking over the "Doubloon chapter" in *Moby Dick* and became aware that people describing images often reveal something about themselves. In this chapter, multiple characters inspected the same image (a Doubloon nailed to the mast of the ship), but each character had significantly different explanations of the imagery. Crew members, including captain Ahab, projected their self-perceptions onto the coin. As one crew member after another described the coin, each saw something quite different. With this in mind, Murray developed a standard set of pictures to be used in psychological counseling for people with troubling conditions. Eventually, another psychologist, David McClelland began using another set of pictures, along with a scoring process, and applied it to organizational psychology to boost the effectiveness of healthy people. Results were used to reveal personal preferences, and provide guidance for individuals and groups to increase their business effectiveness. McClelland's approach to the TAT is used in this book and the accompanying workbook.

You tend to do something you want to do. To find out what you really want to do by asking yourself "What do you really want to do?" does not necessarily reveal what you want. Somehow you have to get around the obstacle of your own thought processes so that when you respond you do not respond on what you think others want you to do, or what you might think is the right thing to do at the time. The TAT is a way to get around this obstacle. This test finds what is natural to you since it essentially provides a "blank canvas" and lets you respond in a natural way. The method for scoring the TAT is shown in an accompanying workbook as well as in Appendices 1 and 2 of this book.

This book applies the results of the TAT to circumstances of life. This is done in order to show you how your motives actually make a difference in your behavior. To be a natural at something is to match your natural motives to the opportunities that present themselves to you. To be a natural at something usually leads to a life that is self-fulfilling, self-actualizing, and at times very joyful.

Contents

Chapter 1 Why Motives are Important   1

Chapter 2 Motives Overview   25

Chapter 3 Motives and Leadership   61

Chapter 4 Motives and Careers   101

Chapter 5 Motives and Choices   121

Chapter 6 Motive Syndromes and Group Identity   149

Chapter 7 Overall Analysis – Putting it Together   171

Appendix 1 Short Motives Assessments
with Example   203

Appendix 2 Motive Training   245

Chapter 1

Why Motives are Important

"To live a fulfilled life, we need to keep creating the "what is next" of our lives."

Mark Twain

This book is about who you are, both who you think you are and who you are naturally. Knowing yourself is a great step in self-actualization, and being "all you can be." Many times, this leads to self-improvement resulting in a more inspired and enjoyable life. You may see this in others when they seem to either inspire those around them, or to watch as opportunities for a better life pass them by. What is need to reach a more fulfilling life through self-awareness can be honed down into four steps.

1. Choose more self-awareness
2. Be aware of the advantages of more self-awareness
3. Know what can be done to reach more self-awareness
4. Examine how motives play a fundamental role in self-awareness

Within step four we will look at why it is important to know your motives, and how motives and opportunities can lead to experiencing your full Behavior Potential which is everything you have the potential to do. There are a variety of ways to think about motives and motivation and these will be briefly addressed. We shall review four foundational motives namely; *achievement, affiliation, power,* and *personal causation.* These will be described, and will function as the basis for examining natural and other behaviors. A combination of motives, known as Motive Syndromes, will be applied throughout the book to show how the things we may be engaged in, such as careers and leadership, can be understood in terms of motives.

Expanding on Self-awareness

Step 1
Choosing More Self-awareness

With so many things to do with your energy, seriously choosing to examine your self-awareness is needed in order that your daily activities do not drive out the opportunity.

Step 2
Advantages of Self-Awareness

Self-awareness can result in experiencing life in very positive ways. You can enhance your self-development, be creative and productive, have fresh ideas, take more pride in your work, develop more self-control, make better decisions, and communicate with others more effectively. Self-awareness can enhance every experience you have, realistically evaluate yourself, come to better social awareness and empathy toward others, and manage relationships better.

With self-awareness you can be more self-reflective by realizing you are the thinker behind the thought, know your standards, and be more focused on the standards rather than yourself thus avoiding holding yourself to impossibly high standards. Have a sense of purpose with personal goals, come to focus on the journey, and feeling one with the world, living in the moment.

Being more self-aware you can have more peak experiences where you have feelings of intense ecstasy, joy, and wonder, realize the importance of your life's activities and your unique value, and come to accept yourself and others as they are while being free of guilt. To realize these positive life experiences means you will need to take action toward self-improvement.

Step 3
Realizing Self-awareness

These are things you can do to enhance your self-awareness and they include:

Creating space and time for self-reflection
Practicing being in the moment
Journaling
Being a good listener
Gaining a different perspective of yourself
Revealing your natural and cognitive motives

Creating Space and Time for Self-Reflection

Plan and follow through on times of solitude. These could be within a day, week, month, or year.

The time between your solitude experiences can have an impact on their value. Longer times between solitude experiences should include a serious inventory of your life place – your family relationships, kinds of friends, job importance, and what could be called your way-of-life. Shorter timeframes between them means coming to a realization of who you are as life unfolds, your behavior concerning personal standards and ethics as they occur daily or episodically in treatment of others.

<u>Practicing Being in the Moment</u>

Pay attention to your inner state. Be aware of your emotions so you can appropriately manage them. There is an appropriate time for almost any emotion. Circumstances should dictate the best way to manage emotions. These emotions could include joy at a wedding, sorrow at a funeral, frustration at a failed activity, or anger at the misuse of charitable contributions, among others.

Besides emotions you have in the moment, you may be concentrating on an activity, learning, or practicing a skill, deeply thinking about something, being creative, trying to impress others, working on a long-term goal, or pushing to complete something. Being in the moment could be having a sense of comfort, or experiencing intuitive self-satisfaction (in the flow of an activity).

<u>Journaling</u>

A journal has been found to be eight times more effective for self-awareness than simply thinking about yourself. Take time at least once a week to record stand-out instances of your inner state. You may use bullet points, short sentences, or a more complete narrative. Do not be concerned over grammar or correct spelling, simply write down, or key in, what stands out to you since your last journal entry. For monthly or quarterly journals take time to go back and review them. Make notes in or around your entries evaluating their positive and negative impacts to you as a person.

Once a year re-read your journal and look for comprehensive indicators of like positive and negative impacts. Decide how to continue the positive and reduce the negative results. Be aware of the people and circumstances that have made a difference on your inner state as you lived over the last year.

You may also share your journal, along with your interpretations, with a spouse or close friend. Discuss with them their agreements or disagreements. Make sure this is a closed-ended meeting taking no more than an hour. The focus of your journal is you and your inner state.

Being a Good Listener

Have focused attention without judging. Good listening is made difficult because of other things going on at the same time, either within the environment or within the minds of those interacting. Some conversations may need to be held in a private environment. Perhaps to deliver extra good or bad messages, or to clear up previous misunderstandings.

The test of a good listener is to be able to repeat what the person or other people have said. Repeating back what you heard, for clarification, is a good technique. For instance, say "Let me see if I understand..." then repeat what you heard. With a more formal dialog you may want to take notes of the conversation. Sometimes it may be appropriate to have questions or probing ideas ready ahead of time. They should act as a script for you but they should not outweigh the dialog taking place as the other person interacts naturally. For a special noteworthy interaction take a few minutes afterward and jot down ideas that came from it.

Gaining a Different Perspective

Increasing self-awareness can come from ideas and opinions of other people. Ask them how they see your behavior. This could be after interacting with others in social environments, after business meetings, or as you are one-on-one with a spouse or close and trusted friend. Ask a question such as, "How do you see me handling my life situations?"

Also, use the feedback from journal examinations, as noted above, to look at yourself through other's eyes. Feedback can also come from others using questionnaires after sessions you have led. An outside view can confirm or awaken a new perspective on who you really are.

Revealing your natural and cognitive motives

Motives can explain why you have a long-term tendency to act in certain ways or have a deep interest in something. They reveal to you the basis of who you are or who your think you are. Motives knowledge provide the most powerful insight into your self-awareness. This book is devoted to providing you that insight by examining your motives and their applications in your life.

Enhancing self-awareness is possible through these efforts of creating space and time for solitude, practicing being in the moment, journaling, being a good listener, gaining a different perspective of yourself, and most importantly revealing your motives. With an increase in self-awareness a more positive life experience will result.

Step 4
Examine Motives

Some activities in life seem both natural and very rewarding at the same time. Often these activities are jobs or professions which suit you, sometimes they are groups that you enjoy as a member, and perhaps they are a hobby or pastime that you find self-rewarding. You feel good when you are engaged in them and often lose track of time. People are sometimes described by others as "naturals" in what they do. It could be about a truck driver, a waitress, a computer programmer, a musician, a manager, a model boat builder, a bowler, or a card player. In other words, any situation where the person and activity are aligned and just seem made for each other. If you are a natural for an activity there is something about you that can make you gravitate, lock into, or be compatible with it. In another vein you may be reminded of a job or task which just did not seem to fit you. You watched the clock or tried to distract yourself with other thoughts. You do not mind changing a flat tire on the car, but would not want to do it as a fulltime job. You might even find tinkering on a car interesting but quickly wear out on the activity. You do not mind buying a car, but you do not look forward to the negotiation that has to happen with the seller, and would never consider a regular job selling cars. You might even say "selling cars is not my forte." If you are not a natural at selling cars, then, in what activities are you a natural? And what could it mean to you to find out?

The overlap of opportunities that you face along with things that you are able to do, represent your Behavior Potential. Behavior Potential covers everything you have the opportunity to do, however there is a special case of activities within your

Behavior Potential where activities that you do provide a feeling of well-being in doing them; this is called the sweet zone. Sweet zones are a manifestation of a natural motive. In fact, what you tend to actually do, when you have a choice of what to do, is a product of your opportunities and your natural motives. When your activities lie within the sweet zone of your Behavior Potential, and you become aware of this fact, it is as if someone has opened the door and revealed to you a life that is rich in self-fulfillment, thereby making you feel you are living a life you have always wanted. People who are self-fulfilled become aware that their motives match their opportunities. They may have come to this realization by the school of Hard Knocks, through trial and error until their activities seemed self-fulfilling or natural, or through a method of self-examination.

This book provides a method for you to align your opportunities with your natural motives, to realize self-fulfillment by revealing your natural motives, and to see how these natural motives engage in life's various opportunities. Alignment can be from modifying your personal natural motives to be compatible with what you are able to do, or from taking advantage of opportunities that fit your personal natural motives. You will learn how it may be possible to effectively engage in tasks you have always wanted to perform, find satisfaction in a career that you have always wanted, be able to lead others, make more effective decisions, and become at ease as a member of various groups.

Behavior Potential

Behavior Potential is all the possible actions you can take in the circumstance in which you are found. Each person brings to circumstances their capacities, knowledge, skills, and gifts. All that you have as a person plus the opportunities present in your environment constitute your Behavior Potential.

Imagine you are stranded on a small sandy desert island, and the only thing on the island is a tree. Your Behavior Potential is fairly limited. You can dig in the sand, you can walk out into the water, you can sit in the shadow of the tree, or you can sit in the exposure of the sun. Now, suppose a beach ball was left out in the ocean and it washes up on the shore of the desert island. You now have an increased Behavior Potential. In addition to all you could do before, you can now pick the ball up, throw the ball in the air, bounce the ball across the sand, throw it out into the ocean and see if it comes back. Suppose while digging in the sand you find an axe and a butane lighter. If you have the ability, you can chop the tree down and start a signal fire with the butane lighter found with the axe. If you had the capacity to fly, you could escape the island by flight and land near a restaurant off the mainland shore for a bite to eat. Alas, you do not have that capacity since you are a human and not a bird. Behavior Potential is a function of capacity, opportunity, knowledge, skills and gifts. The desire to act on Behavior Potential comes from personal natural motives. If you did not want to get off the island, you would not take advantage of opportunities such as digging and finding an axe and lighter, or setting a signal fire.

I am reminded of the movie *Cast Away* with Tom Hanks. In the movie his Behavior Potential was fairly low when he first washed up upon the island. As time went on and other items washed up on the island as well, his Behavior Potential increased and he used his ability, knowledge, and gifts to find a way to free himself from the confines of the island. Key to his survival was his motive to overcome odds and to meet the goal of freeing himself from the island. He was a "natural" to survive because of his *achievement* motive. He used this *achievement* motive for setting and achieving goals, he had learned somewhere in his life, to help him become successful at his job with FedEx. Without the motive to spark action, opportunities to realize your Behavior Potential would be ignored, and your life would not be as satisfying or fulfilling as it could be. Tom Hanks' character would have been stuck on the island never to see his homeland again.

In another example, *It's a Wonderful Life* we see that opportunity, capacity, knowledge, and skills come together for a fulfilling life for a film character. George Bailey, the main character played by Jimmy Stewart, finds himself in a situation where his natural inclinations (his personal natural motives) to help others, and developing friendships with people in town including people in trouble, is compatible with the opportunities presented to him when his father is no longer able to manage the Bailey's Savings Loan, and George has to take over. The opportunity combined with his knowledge and abilities is compatible with his position as manager of the Savings and Loan. George's natural care for people and his desire to control situations to help people fits the opportunity that comes along for management of the Saving and Loan. His motives led to acting in the sweet zone of his Behavior Potential leading to a life that was self-fulfilling. When he wishes he had never been born, and the angel makes this wish come true, he sees the impact his life has had on others. When he discovers his friends really matter and his care of others has made his life fulfilling, he begs for his life to return to normal. The movie ends with him being saved from financial ruin by all the friends he had made during his life, along with him realizing how fulfilling his life had been. Once again, we see opportunity compatible with personal natural motives to produce a fulfilling life. George Bailey realizes he has actually lived in the sweet zone of his Behavior Potential as someone who naturally cares for others, and is able to make solid friendships. George Bailey's motive of *affiliation* with people is distinctly different from the motive of *achievement* exhibited by Tom Hanks' character.

Suppose you have grown up all your life from grade school through high school desiring to be a teacher. So, you enroll in college with an education major allowing you to become certified as a teacher in your state. After successfully completing all the coursework, in your senior year you are required to complete a practicum which will put you in a real classroom with real students. You are placed in a classroom with third grade students, and the teacher there provides you the opportunity to take over the classroom two days a week. After several weeks in the classroom, you discover that the control it takes to teach a third-grade class or an elementary school class gives you pause. You quickly learn that having to control them to work in class, and encourage them to do their homework is not something you really want to do. The power it takes to control a classroom and deal with all the other people such as parents and school administrators, is not something for which you have bargained. It would have been very beneficial before starting a career as a teacher to find out if you have the necessary natural *power* motive to be comfortable leading and controlling a classroom. Teaching is more about power and creativity, as found in the *power* and in the *personal causation* motives, than being friends with the students and parents as in the *affiliation* motive. Motives can be discovered through self-assessment and counseling using an organized method. If you are prepared to do something, and the opportunity to do that activity is present, you can gain insight into your natural motives based on how you perform that activity. If

11

natural motives are not present, there is no resultant feeling of natural fulfillment, and it may even be stressful for you. Acting outside of the sweet zone of your Behavior Potential is unnatural. Natural motives are what make the sweet zone possible.

Knowing your natural motives and awareness of how they fit with your opportunities result in a life that is self-fulfilling. Imagine experiencing a way of life, a career, a job, or a social environment that is most natural to you, where you not only feel good but perform at your best level. Every situation provides a variety of opportunities to act or avoid. Given all the things you could do in a situation, you will gravitate to those you find self-rewarding or natural. You may be interested in something but lack the ability to act on it so the opportunity is missed. You may also be interested in something but lack the motives to inspire actions to do it. However, if you are interested in something and have the ability and the requisite knowledge to act on it, and you find acting on it self-fulfilling and pleasant, this would demonstrate how you were inspired to act from your natural motives. Natural motives are the tendency to act on opportunities that present themselves to you. However, some opportunities do not fit your motives still you may yet act on them, but without producing a feeling of self-satisfaction and joy.

As an example, Gerry is interested in acquiring more master chess points, in learning and being able to cook French cuisine, in planning trips with location and time constraints, and in putting together neighborhood block parties. These activities are founded on his desire to set up and overcome internal goals. Goal attainment is key to the *achievement* motive (described later). Being able to act from the sweet zone of Behavior Potential comes from the marriage of opportunities that present themselves along with one's natural motive (see Figure 1-1).

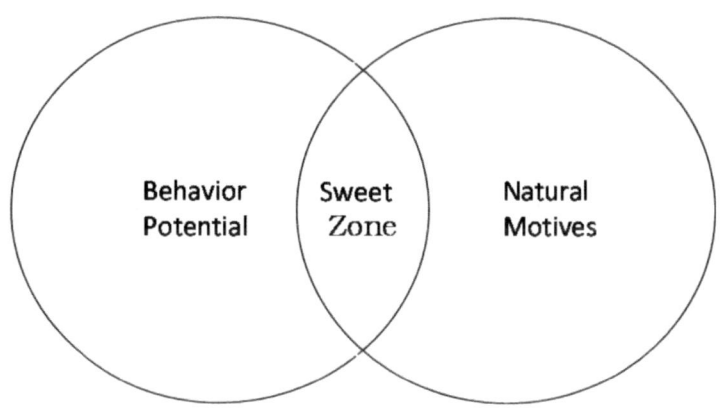

Behavior Potential Sweet Zone
Figure 1-1

Natural motives are the basis of your desires or wants. They supply the personal energy to act on your capacities, talents, and gifts. When properly aligned they can have a positive impact on performing a task, on building a career, on acting as a leader, on making decisions, or on being a part of a group. When opportunities, capacities, talents, and gifts are compatible with your natural motives, you are able to move forward in a smooth, confident way with little hesitation and personal doubt. At other times you may find yourself on the precipice of moving forward but cannot quite do it. Hesitation and doubt occur when your natural motives are not compatible with what you are trying to do. You may even find yourself trying to perform a task you really want to do but cannot quite seem to find the time or energy to do it. You find yourself not being able to comfortably perform in a career that seemed perfect when you started. You are ill at ease in leading a team, on edge trying to make decisions, or feel uncomfortable in being a part of a group. A life lived with unrealized natural motives can be tough, and lead to finding ways to escape this lack of fulfillment, such as job hopping, constant vacationing, persistently changing hobbies, moving residences and locations often, and constantly searching for other best-friend relationships. **Discovering one's natural motives and how they might fit within life's opportunities is a key to self-fulfillment and a fuller life.**

You act within the sweet zone of your Behavior Potential when your personal natural motives and behavioral opportunities are compatible. This compatibility can be accomplished by either recognizing the personal natural motives you have and adjusting what you do or adjusting your personal natural motives. When there is compatibility between the opportunities you act on and your natural motives, you experience personal self-fulfillment.

Ways People Think about Motives

Motives or motivations are often characterized as reasons for what we do, or do not do. Nancy was motivated to get that job. The Panthers won the game because they were really motivated. "I can't seem to get anything done; I just don't seem to be motivated." "Wow, that was a great motivating speech!" "You need to get your staff motivated to get this project done." All these comments show the variety of ways people use the word motivation as a trigger for immediate action. But they do not explain why someone has a long-term tendency to act in a certain way or is deeply interested in something. People can admit to a tendency to act, but often cannot describe these tendencies as reasons but merely feelings. Motives, when identified and understood, can reveal reasons why people tend to act in certain ways over long periods of time.

Motives in Your Life

When acted on these motives can produce behaviors that are self-fulfilling. That is, they can be described as producing self-actualization or self-awareness. They do not satisfy social pressures to make others accept you or make you feel good or avoid painful or unwanted results. They are about how you prefer to act. Nor are they usually emotionally charged actions resulting from what is commonly attributed to a motivational speaker. These motives are dispositions that an individual has acquired over time. They are stimulated when an opportunity to act is compatible with them. Someone with an *achievement* motive (internal desire to overcome a goal – see below) might find it difficult to not accept the opportunity of a challenge like hitting a golf ball a great distance, or getting ready for work in record time, or getting a new book read by the end of the week. Self-actualizing or self-fulfilling behaviors are very individualistic and depend on internal motives.

Your current motives connect to something that you inherently find significant, and this significance is learned through a history of reinforced behaviors. "I like to play golf because I have learned that being out on the course with friends gives me a sense of personal fulfillment and kinship with others." My golf behavior is reinforced by the fulfillment derived from it. Golf has a significance in my life that it may not have for someone else. Motives are the learned determinates for tendencies to act or behave in certain ways. In understanding your motives, you can explain why some things you do bring self-fulfillment while others just bring drudgery to your life. Knowing your motives will make it easier to live positively with those things that are natural to you, as well as live through those things that are not.

Four Meaningful Motives

Four motives are particularly relevant for understanding the significance of what we tend to do. These motives have been studied and used over many years and have proven successful in describing why people tend to act in certain ways and not others. They can be used to explain why we have certain tendencies or interests in life. These four motives are *achievement, affiliation, power,* and *personal causation.* Aligning these motives with opportunities has been proven successful in improving outcomes for individuals and groups. Research has shown people with the *achievement* motive have performed better in business performance. Those with the *power* motive have had a more positive impact on their leadership. Those with the *affiliation* motive have been able to work more effectively with others. Those with the *personal causation* motive have been able to have positive impact on how others behave. Motives have a positive impact on behavior when the opportunities to act are aligned with them. Further, knowing your motives can provide information on what opportunities would be most natural for you.

Achievement

Someone with a well-developed *achievement* motive would have a tendency or perhaps even a need to overcome self-imposed goals of excellence, to accomplish tasks and jobs that present an above-normal degree of difficulty, or to overcome pressures to secure an effective outcome. These people are challenge-oriented. You can see people challenge their own performance by increasing their energy to do better in a sport, a job, or updating their home.

Some people may like to play golf because they are goal oriented. They may be challenged to beat their last score, shoot better than par, or defeat opponents in a tournament. Tom Hanks in *Cast Away* shows his natural tendency to achieve and overcome the difficult goal of surviving and finding a way off the island. He comes to the island having already learned and developed it through his life circumstances, particularly his challenging job with FedEx. He developed the *achievement* motive previously through his own activities, so when an *achievement* situation presents itself, he acts accordingly.

Affiliation

With the *affiliation* motive, a person is concerned with establishing, maintaining, or growing relationships with another person or people. They are people-oriented and go out of their way to initiate, grow, or maintain relationships with others.

Golf might be enjoyed because of the significance attached to developing and/or maintaining friendships. George Bailey in *It's a Wonderful Life* presents a good picture of someone high in the *affiliation* motive. He goes out of his way to make friends with people who need a friend or who need help.

Power

A person with the *power* motive looks to control situations. The positive side of *power* refers to using power for the good of people in a situation and as addressed in this book. Conversely, the negative side of power is often what we take as "power hungry" or power for one's own good frequently at the expense of others. Often a person uses wise counsel to get others to understand or see the necessity, either good or bad, of working toward an outcome. They influence situations and the people in them for a social positive outcome. *Power* can also show up as the desire to make an impact on people and their community either through individual acts or through life-long pursuits.

One might like to play golf because there is satisfaction from setting up a league, from being in charge of a regular golf outing, or from playing with the objective or intent of becoming the star of the league. George Bailey is another fine example of someone with a high *power* motive. He desires to improve the lives of people living in his community through actions taken by the Bailey Savings and Loan. He has the skill and talent to use money from the Savings and Loan so people may build their own houses and enjoy a better way of life than they would otherwise have. In a previous example being an elementary school teacher requires control of a classroom and would be compatible with someone high in the power motive.

Personal Causation

People high in the *personal causation* motive prefer self-reliance and being an initiator of their own behavior, not being a pawn of someone else. They take it upon themselves to initiate actions where these actions are not a response to someone else being an initiator.

Golf appeals to these people since it involves self-initiative in choosing how each shot is played or when and where to play. Tom Hanks demonstrates the personal causation motive through creativity, initiating his own actions to survive and escape from the island.

These four motives can be combined in various ways to drive and orient behavior producing tendencies to act or think in certain ways. Many times, what you really want to do, when it is just up to you, can be explained by these motives. They become affective determinants of your behavior. These motives do not absolutely control one's behavior, but they do orient interests, and when compatible with opportunities, they can produce feelings of satisfaction and personal fulfillment. Motives are at the heart of what we find interesting.

Motive Syndromes

A motive syndrome is a single motive or a set of motives that describe motive behaviors. Within the four motives, there are motive-level combinations that provide insight into behavioral opportunities you may face. In the example with Tom Hanks' character in *Cast Away* we see him acting with a motive syndrome that combines the *achievement* motive with the *personal causation* motive; this is labelled Overcomer syndrome. With Jimmy Stewart's character in the movie, *It's a Wonderful Life* there is a combination of the *affiliation* motive and *power* motive producing the Persuader syndrome. Persuader engages his character in opportunities to both form friendships and to manage the Savings and Loan for the good of others. He uses money from the Savings and Loan to help people in his community build their first home.

In this book there are motive syndromes identified across a variety of life situations. The syndromes differ somewhat across these life situations as well as how they are labelled. Using different syndromes and their labels across the life situations allow us to make them more informative within the life situation. For instance, leadership syndromes such as Influencer and Ambassador are more informative for leadership, syndromes for careers such as Mutuality and Directing relate better to that life situation. Personality assessments are employed widely and for various reasons. Treating them as another life circumstance is helpful in revealing their assumed motives position. They are each fundamentally based on motives. Personality motive syndromes are shown across various

19

assessment approaches, thus showing how motives are the basis for each approach. Subsequently, motive syndromes are used within each of the life situations of Leadership, Careers, Decision Making, and Groups. By identifying your personal natural motives and motive syndromes, it is possible to be informed of your personality as taken across various personality assessments, what your most compatible leadership approach would be, your most compatible career, your natural decision making approach, and what kinds of groups you would find most satisfying.

Ten motive syndromes are identified below in Figure 1-2. The ten motive syndromes of Persuader, Doer, Initiator, Overcomer, Socializer, Agent, Actioner, Originator, Dominator, and Empathizer each have one or two predominant, or high motives associated with them. While each situational opportunity will have its own set of motive syndromes; Leadership has its own, Careers has its own, Decision Making has its own, and Groups has its own. The following motive syndromes will be used throughout the book to provide a consistent viewpoint. Examples are taken from those presented above about Jimmy Stewart and Tom Hanks. Margaret Thatcher and Eleanor Roosevelt are explained in Chapter 3. Cosmo Kramer from the television show *Seinfeld* is an example of someone who has both *achievement* in mind as indicated by his constant looking to do something different or better, but can't seem to do it without his other friends. He has the strong *achievement* and strong *affiliation* motives. The example of Dorothy from *The Wizard of Oz* represents someone who has both *power* and pers*onal causation* as indicated when she is creative along with controlling those around her; namely, the tin man, the lion, and the scarecrow. Her *power* motive comes out when she feels the need to control them for their own. She also has to be creative, as in perso*nal causation,* to find their way to the emerald city.

Those with a single motive are a bit different since they are driven by one primary idea. In the case of the Actioner, this is someone who leaps before they look. When there is something that needs accomplishing, they take action right away. Hence the *achievement* name is Gary the Leaper. Someone who has a single predominant motive of *affiliation* is an Empathizer and is identified here with an *affiliation* name Joan the Helper. No matter what happens in the situation Joan will be there to help even when it may cause problems for herself or other people. Usually, she will be called on to assist in a situation because she will seldom turn down a request for help. Someone with a single predominant motive of *power* is called Dominator here, and is labelled with the *power* name Larry the Organizer. This is the person who looks at the situation with the people in it and organizes actions so that everyone would benefit no matter what. That is, in some cases there may be better individual actions for the people, but Larry only sees what they can do together since it has to be done in an organized way. Someone with a single predominant motive of *personal causation* or Originator is labelled with the *personal causation* name Betsy the Primer. She is ready to take the next step once it is understood how it would impact the world around her as well as the people. She does not wait to find out what others have done; she initiates her own activities to make sure the outcome is positive.

Syndrome	Example	Motives			
		Ach	Affil	Pow	Pers Caus
Persuader	Jimmy Stewart in *It's a Wonderful Life*		High	High	
Doer	Margaret Thatcher (Chapter 3)	High		High	
Initiator	Eleanor Roosevelt (Chapter 3)		High		High
Overcomer	Tom Hanks in *Cast Away*	High			High
Socializer	Cosmo Kramer in *Seinfeld*	High	High		
Agent	Dorothy In *The Wizard of Oz*			High	High
Actioner	Gary the Leaper	High			
Empathizer	Joan the Helper		High		
Dominator	Larry the Organizer			High	
Originator	Betsy the Primer				High

Motive Syndromes
Figure 1-2

Each chapter in this book uses a different set of motive syndromes that are more descriptive of the application of the four foundational motives. Consider their descriptive labels as a more detailed expression of the overall motive syndromes provided in this chapter. (See Figure 1-3.)

Syndromes / Motives	Persuader	Doer	Initiator	Overcomer	Socializer	Agent	Actioner	Empathizer	Dominator	Originator
General Chapter 1	Persuader	Doer	Initiator	Overcomer	Socializer	Agent	Actioner	Empathizer	Dominator	Originator
Classic Trait Behavior Chapter 2	Choleric	Melancholic	Sanguine	Phlegmatic	NA	NA	NA	NA	NA	NA
Leadership Chapter 3	Influencer	Mover	Ambassador	Innovator	NA	NA	NA	NA	NA	NA
Careers Chapter 4	Controlling	Directing	Initiating	Initiating	Mutuality	Leading	Directing Somewhat	Coordinating	Directing Somewhat	Initiating Somewhat
Choices Chapter 5	Consider Sensitivities	Influence to a Result	Work Around Sensitivities	Get it Right no Matter	Push Through Sensitivities	Reality Influence	Get it Done	Adjust to Values	Sensitively Influence	Get it Creatively
Groups Chapter 6	Sensitive	Controlling	Tactful	Insistent	Candid	Performance	Immediate	Moral	Influential	Creative
Achievement		High	High	High			High			
Affiliation	High		High		High			High		
Power	High	High				High			High	
Personal Causation		High		High		High				High

All Motive Syndromes
Figure 1-3

Motives in Your Life

The overall outcome for taking time to identify and examine your motives, a well as motive syndromes, is to find compatibility with your natural inclinations and the behavioral opportunities that come along in your life. Your natural motives are often different from what you would report as your motives if someone asked you. Due to activities of the day, you may be unaware or only marginally aware of your natural motives. A method of identifying your natural motives will be addressed later in this book along with how they differ from your self-reported motives. Natural motives are what allow you to perform from the sweet zone of your Behavior Potential. The alignment and compatibility of your motive syndromes with the opportunities that present themselves will lead to a more fulfilling life producing a degree of satisfaction, a feeling of pleasure, and a sense of self-realization. In short, knowing your natural motives and how they connect to the opportunities in your life can make you a better person.

Chapter 2

Motives Overview

All I really want to do is, baby, be friends with you
                                        B. Dylan

Understanding people and their behavior has been examined from various points of view and has grown more sophisticated over the years. Several time-honored approaches will be reviewed along with how people generally think about themselves and the concepts of motives and motivation. These will include the classical model, the Jungian model, Temperaments, and the Dimensional model.

Two assessment methods will be highlighted to provide an understanding of one's motives. One method is cognitive and uses a multiple-choice questionnaire, and the other method is natural and elicits free-flowing responses to neutral cues. Cognitive assessments reveal what we think about ourselves, while natural assessments reveal what we actually are.

Four individual motives are assessed and combined in ways that form motive syndromes. While there are other motives that can be described, the four motives of *achievement, affiliation, power,* and *personal causation* provide a consistent foundation for understanding tendencies to act and have proven over time to explain behavioral outcomes.

How motives are learned is discussed as a natural incentive-based process that occurs over time in ordinary ways. Motives can also be learned through a classroom situation using appropriate exercises and examples. Whether you learn in a natural way or through classroom experiences, it is possible to become a master of your motives potentially opening the door to significant life self-fulfillment.

Motives, while important, are not the only things which are the basis of human behavior. Motives will be applied into the concept of the whole person in order to make distinctions between motives and other characteristics of a person. We begin with the Person Concept.

The Person Concept

Identifying and understanding your motives can give you the power to reach for something in life that you may have always desired. Unexpectedly you may find motives that reveal aspirations you might now seek. Motives can set people off on journeys of personal discovery and illumination. You can see possibilities that were hidden before, by envisioning the world in a new way, and, to even be set free from entanglements that can bind a life into "same-old, same-olds." Actions resulting from motive awareness can lead to new jobs or careers and new or renewed relationships, along with new ways of understanding how life and things in life actually work. To help understand ways in which motives fit into our behavior, I shall turn to the *person concept* as put forward in the works on Descriptive Psychology.

Descriptive Psychology is a sort of bookkeeping construct for behavior. It provides conceptual access to what makes up a person, namely, the person concept if you will. A person can be described as having attitudes, traits, interests, and styles. Attitudes are temporary and require a target or object – as in one has an attitude toward something, someone, or even an idea. As an example, one might develop an attitude about Betsy due to how she embarrassed you in the meeting. Traits are permanent (though changeable over time) and are consistent across circumstances; they provide the data others use to know us. For instance, Dan never seems to pass a dog without petting it and even speaking to it. One could conclude that Dan has a dog lover trait. Interests need objects, specifically, if one is interested in something. As an example, Leo goes bowling every Friday night and would not miss it for the world. Leo has an interest in bowling. Styles are how life is accommodated independent of circumstances and usually of little consequence. As an example, Larry always opens all his mail before he reads any of it.

Among the elements used to describe a person, interests are at the heart of motives. An interest is necessary for you to actually engage in an activity – if you had no interest, you would not do it. However, interests do not necessarily produce an activity but may just be a tendency to act in certain ways. It is the motivational component of interests that make them different from attitudes and traits. Motive awareness can facilitate taking deliberate action for personal growth. Motives are a natural part of each person; they are internal tendencies to act. They essentially apply an internal criterion to what the environment presents leading to a tendency to act. See Figure 2-1.

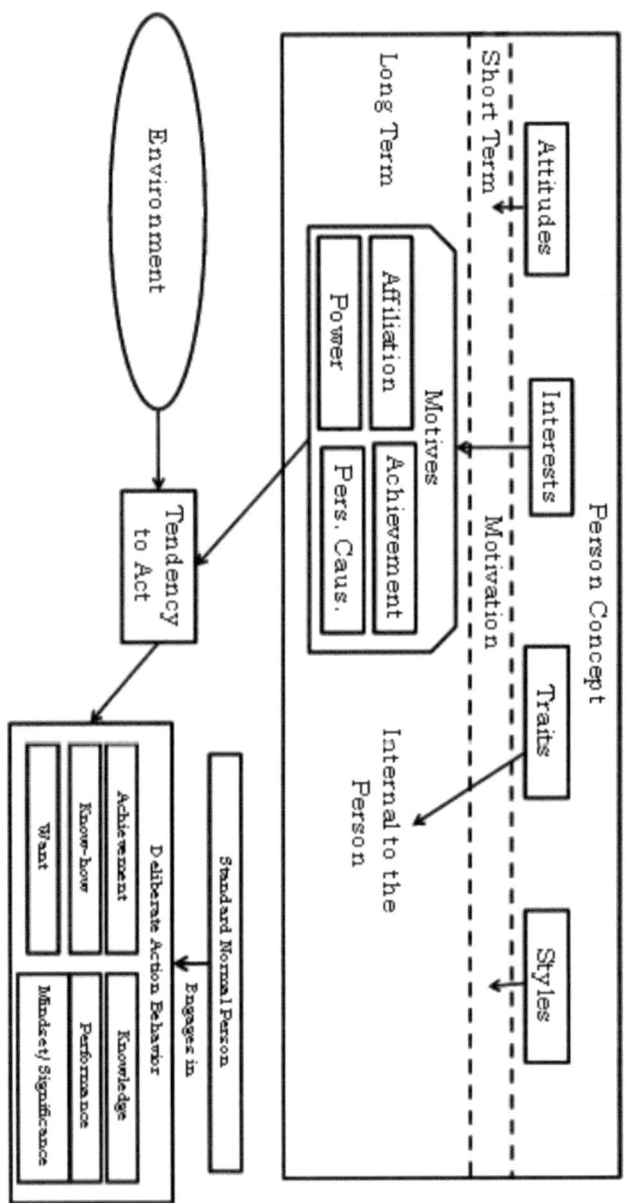

Figure 2-1
The Person Concept and Motives

Understanding Differences in People and Motive Syndromes

Motives are foundational for understanding many formal explanations of behavior. Have you ever been acquainted with someone who seems to act just like someone else you know? "Marg and Lois are just alike. Every time we..." Some people seem to possess the same traits as others, and if we look at everyone we know, perhaps we can categorize them into certain types or kinds. We can take a look at various ways that people have developed to understand, characterize and possibly predict a person's behavior. We develop an understanding of how the four significant motives *achievement, affiliation, power,* and *personal causation* are foundational to our understanding of behavior. Motives can be useful in explaining individual differences by combining them to produce a set of motive personality syndromes. In the case of understanding individual differences in personality a set of six syndromes are produced by taking groups of two motives from the four foundational motives. A summary of the six syndromes for all the personality approaches in this chapter will be provided after all the personalities are reviewed. We have already seen a sneak preview of the six types of motive syndromes in Figure 1-2 from Chapter 1.

Classical Analysis

For over 2,000 years people have been trying to understand people by categorizing them in various ways. Hippocrates in 370 BC theorized that human behaviors are based on four separate temperaments associated with four fluids or "humors" of the body. These humors are *choleric* temperament (yellow bile from the liver), *melancholic* temperament (black bile from the kidneys), *sanguine* temperament (red blood from the heart), and *phlegmatic* temperament (white phlegm from the lungs).

Much later the Greek physician and philosopher Galen built on Hippocrates's theory. He conjectured that differences in people could be explained by their humors, and each person exhibits one of the four temperaments. For example, the *choleric* person is passionate, ambitious, and bold, indicative of the *affiliation* and *power* motives; the *melancholic* person is reserved, anxious, and unhappy, indicative of the *achievement* and *power* motives; the *sanguine* person is joyful, eager, and optimistic indicative of the *affiliation* and personal *causation* motives; and the *phlegmatic* person is calm, reliable, and thoughtful, indicative of the *achievement* and *personal causation* motives. Galen's theory was prevalent for over 1,000 years.

Later, building upon Galen's ideas, it was suggested people traits could be understood using two major axes: emotional/non-emotional and changeable/unchangeable. One axis separates strong emotions (*melancholic* and *choleric)* from weak emotions (*phlegmatic* and *sanguine*). The other axis divided changeable temperaments (*choleric* and *sanguine*) from unchangeable ones (*melancholic* and *phlegmatic*). See Figure 2-2.

Motives in Your Life

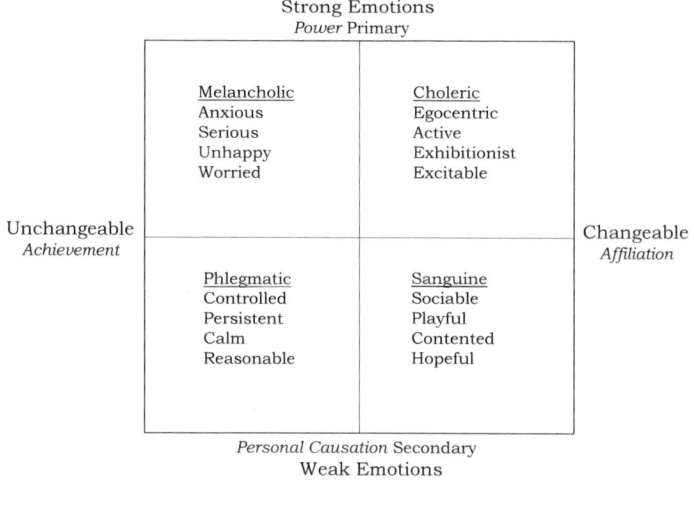

These fluids are a way of understanding people independent of their circumstances. They identify certain traits for an individual. A motive analysis of these traits provides a "motive syndrome" for the trait using the four motives of *achievement, affiliation, power,* and *personal causation.* Motive syndromes are formed by looking at two predominant motives, and these syndromes can therefore be used across various traits or personality approaches. When you know the motive syndromes of a trait, the syndrome provides a more profound look into the trait along with information to change it if desired. In using personality fluids as a guide, strong emotions are explained by a concern for *power* while weak emotions are explained by *personal causation.* Unchangeable preference involves pursuing a goal regardless of its personal impact and is provisioned by an *achievement* motive. Changeable demonstrates a concern about impact on people that is serviced by an *affiliation* motive.

Many other trait assessments have been devised over the years. In order to see how deeply influential these motives are from various trait-oriented viewpoints, some of these will be described below, along with their motive syndromes. Motives are truly foundational for these assessments.

| Syndrome (See fig. 1-2) | Classic Trait | Motives | | | |
		Ach	Affil	Pow	Pers Causa
Persuader	Choleric		High	High	
Doer	Melancholic	High		High	
Initiator	Sanguine		High		High
Overcomer	Phlegmatic	High			High
Socializer	Unexamined	High	High		
Agent	Unexamined			High	High

Figure 2-3
Trait/Personality Motive Syndromes

Assessing Motives

Sometimes we rely on others to give us guidance. Often this guidance comes with the help of self-assessment, multiple choice tests that are designed to provide insight into personal preferences. With results from that analysis, your coach, career counselor, or HR specialist can outline activities that are more closely aligned with your motive preferences. These question-answer, or cognitive-based tests as in MBTI® (Myers Briggs Type Indicator), DiSC®, (Dominance, Influence, Steadiness, and Conscientiousness) provide information about what we <u>think</u> of ourselves, or possibly what we want others to think about us, and not what may be natural preferences. Your responses come from a thoughtful and reasoned self-examination that can be influenced by others through cultural standards, or personal expectations of those around you.

Measuring natural motives is founded upon the idea that when people are asked to be creative, they will rely on their natural motives (sometimes called their motive dispositions). When individuals are shown a neutral picture and asked to describe it by a story, they respond according to their natural motives (unless they have reasons to be unresponsive in the assessment). The stories are written responses to the questions: What is happening? Who are the people? What happened before? What are the people thinking about and feeling? What do they want? What will happen next? The stories are scored for four motives using the scoring standards of the Thematic Apperception Test (TAT). This is a well-established methodology to analyze the subject's story that reveals their underlying motives, concerns, and the way they see the social world. A*chievement, affiliation, power,* and *personal causation* are the four measured motives (described earlier).

These four motives can also be assessed from answers to written questions as opposed to stories. Answers to specific questions are cognitive/thought responses for what an individual <u>thinks</u> of themselves, and not necessarily how they would <u>naturally</u> respond. Research has shown that the same motive assessed in these two ways does not necessarily correlate. The natural responses and the cognitive-based responses provide different information about the same motives. The natural responses, derived from a neutral picture, reveal inherent preferences, while the cognitive-based responses are an individual's self-perception to a specific question. Of course, self-perception is what one thinks their

33

motives to be, but what one thinks can be influenced by what one believes to be a culturally good response, or even what they think the testing situation implies would be the "best" response. The two assessments reveal what one perceives themselves to be along with their natural inclinations.

When one examines what they think they want, alongside natural preferences, they discover reasons for productive/unproductive behaviors as well as personal feelings of satisfaction/dissatisfaction. This comparison between natural and self-perceived motives can provide a basis for personal improvement by revealing the need for motives training, coaching, or both. Motives training and coaching are useful for increasing leadership effectiveness, enhancing job satisfaction, and providing personal life-satisfaction.

<u>Cognitive Assessment of Motives</u>

Assessing motives cognitively involves asking people what they think of themselves through a set of motive questions, as well as what one thinks interests them. This self-perception provides useful information on what people think they would do when faced with freedom to choose a course of action. Self-perception is based on a variety of past experiences, not only what would come naturally. It might derive from what we think others will think of us when we make a choice. Personal and cultural influences in one's life are powerful determinants of what we might consider to be a good choice. Ultimately, when we think we would act in certain ways, we may not actually behave in these ways because it takes too much effort or requires more attention than we are willing to provide. Although we are not naturally driven to act in a certain way, we may have had the experiences that make that way seem the best choice. We may act in an *achievement* way to satisfy an immediate need for money, but would not act that way if the need for money did not exist. In a cognitive assessment, what usually comes out is an amalgam of all past influences wherein the natural response is now masked. If one is brought up and taught that human interactions are the best of all interactions, then answers to the questions below would all tend to be medium or high. This would be 'scored' as a strong *affiliation* motive, a humanistic motive, consistent with being taught to value human interaction. Yet, *affiliation* may not show up as a natural behavior because it has not been built up through personal interactions and experiences.

Basic cognitive assessment of the *affiliation* motive:

Check the rating that best describes you:

Low   Medium   High
_____   _____   _____

1. I make the extra effort to be with my friends

_____   _____   _____

2. I am in my element when I am surrounded by people who not only do their work but really enjoy life

_____   _____   _____

3. I really like the friendships I have developed at work

_____   _____   _____

Natural Motive Assessment

Natural motives are not influenced by a thought process that leads to a self-perceived notion of oneself. Natural motives influence behavior when a person takes a course of action or makes a decision that coincides with their natural interest. A person may play golf out of obligation to satisfy a company demand to participate in a company-sponsored tournament, or they may play as a natural interest rather than a choice influenced by other factors.

Discovering natural motives means assessing someone without forcing on them a response that requires thinking in detail about the response. That is, to move away from what one thinks is natural to what would be more natural. This is done by presenting to the person a neutral prompt, and then having them reflect on this prompt in their own free-flowing words. This can be done by looking at a picture and writing a story through answering questions. The following is a natural assessment example using a picture as the neutral prompt.

Motives in Your Life

Example of a natural motive assessment:

Please look at the picture and answer the following questions.

What is happening?
Who are the people?
What happened before?
What are the people thinking about and feeling?
What do they want?
What will happen next?

.

.

.

(Questions answered here provide the story)

.

.

.

Two actual examples of responses to this prompt follow.

Example 1

It was a beautiful fall day, and Susie came home to visit her father, Bob, from college. They decided to gather up the draft horses so that they could take the wagon out on their property. Her father breeds horses for the AB hitch. Susie misses the horses when she is away at college. Bob loves to get additional training for the horses whenever he can. It was wonderful father/daughter time for Susie and Bob. And Shep the herding dog loved it too. Susie will miss it when she goes back to school but it was just the break she needed from school. Bob will be sad as his little girl is all grown up and doesn't need him.

This story relates a concern for relationships/affiliations. The prompt is neutral and does not suggest relationship, but the story writer projected the feeling of growing or maintaining a relationship.

Example 2 (same prompt, different respondent)

> Marco & Julia are taking a walk through the countryside with their horses Sally & Flower. They also brought along with them their dog Bingo. Marco & Julia are prized vineyard owners, which is located in northern Italy. They are chatting about how they came from nothing and now are living in paradise. This coming year's harvest will be the best ever and they couldn't be happier. They will continue to stroll through their land as the evening approaches and prepare for a party they are hosting tonight. Life is good.

In this second example from the same picture prompt, a concern for *achievement*, striving for a goal or accomplishing a difficult task appears. Once again, the prompt is neutral, but what is revealed in the story is projected out from the writer.

The first story respondent scored low in the question/answer assessment (cognitive assessment) for *affiliation*. What someone thinks they are is not always what naturally comes out. Someone may answer "low" to "medium" for being with friends, liking people at work, and so forth. However, when given a neutral prompt, they come up with affiliative responses. In other words, *affiliation* is natural for them even though they may reason in their own mind that it is not.

Motives from Story Content

Content of stories can be assessed for presence of motives. As indicated above the first respondent was showing the presence of *affiliation*, while the second the presence of *achievement*. The following describes what to look for in a story for each of the four motives. For a complete scoring description, see the companion scoring manual *Understanding Motives* or Appendices 1 or 2.

Achievement Motive Scoring

What one looks for in a story for positive *achievement* imagery is:

A. Competition with a standard of excellence
B. Explicitly stated desire to win (in competitive game)
C. Unique accomplishment, as an example, not run of the mill but something that marks the person as a personal success (inventions, artistic creations), or long-term involvement
D. Long-term achievement goal as being a success in life (becoming a doctor, lawyer, successful businessman).

Affiliation Motive Scoring

What one looks for in the story for affiliative imagery is:

A. Evidence of a concern in one or more of the characters over establishing, maintaining, or renewing a positive affective relationship with another person. The relationship is most often seen as friendly – seeking some form of friendship. Concern is how one feels about the other or their relationship. Statements of

41

being liked, or accepted, or forgiven could be present. Circumstances could be of acceptance, rejection, separation, or some disruption of the relationship (time, space, other priorities in life).

B. Evidence from generally accepted affiliative, compassionate activities such as parties, reunions, visits, or relaxed small talk. Others may be friendly, nurturant acts such as consoling, helping, or being concerned about the happiness or well-being of another. However, these activities should not be scored if they are done out of obligation, or a sense of what is culturally required (e.g. a father protecting his daughter).

Power Motive Scoring

What one looks for in the story for *Power* Imagery (PM) is:

A. Evidence of someone showing power concern through actions that in themselves express power. They can be present, in the past, planned or even fantasized. Some explicit examples include:

a. Giving help, assistance, advice, or support of another (solicited advice is not scored).

b. Trying to control other people through regulating their behavior or conditions of their lives, or seeking information that would affect another's life or actions (searching, investigating, checking up on) such as "They are being sent to get information on other shows."

42

c. Trying to influence, persuade, convince, make a point, or argue with another person.
d. Trying to impress someone or the world at large. Examples are creative writing, making news or publicity, trying to win an election, or any action that will attract widespread attention. "He took her out to make a good impression on her." "He spent most of the day getting ready so he would get a standing ovation."
e. Strong forceful actions that affect others (e.g., reprimands, attacks, verbal insults, assaults); gaining the upper hand; or taking advantage of another's weakness to impose one's will. "I told her to get off the horse even if she wanted to ride more."

B. Someone does something that aroused strong positive or negative emotions in others. Others may feel pleasure, delight, awe, gratitude, anger, jealousy, or expressions of interest. "She told him how she felt and he began to weep."

C. Someone is described as having a concern for reputation or position. The affect should be about public position or prestige. Not scored is something that provides internal satisfaction/dissatisfaction of a private goal. "She was thinking about the impression she had made."

Personal Causation Motive Scoring

Look for someone in the story doing something intentionally to produce a change. The person is acting as an origin or taking initiative, independently determining his/her own goals, freely choosing an activity with which to pursue the goal(s), and being realistic about his/her abilities and relationships with others and the environment. This individual displays self-confidence about his/her ability to initiate successful behavior leading to a positive conclusion to a goal setting sequence. An individual in the story decides to get something or some state of affairs. This cannot be imposed by another agency. Two major components are goal setting sequence and responsibility. If there is no goal setting sequence in the story, then it may still be scored if there is instrumental activity taken by the character on his own and not as a response to someone or something else in the story.

A more complete cognitive and natural motive assessment can be found in Appendices 1 and 2. Also, Appendix 3 shows how to compare the cognitive and the natural assessment scores. There is complete training manual on how to learn and execute assessments in a companion workbook entitled *Understanding Motives: Cognitive and Natural Scoring with the Thematic Apperception Test (TAT).* [Available from the Alberts Adams Institute.]

Differences in Cognitive and Natural Assessments

Results of a cognitive question/answer assessment often differ from a natural assessment. What one thinks of themselves motivationally is not necessarily what one actually is motivated to do given a neutral circumstance. The difference can be explained by how the human brain deals with these assessments. A cognitive assessment is basically asking the respondent to solve a problem, that is, answer a question about themselves. The brain can be described as having three separate locations for handling information. The *executive* center determines what to do or how to solve a problem, the *social* center deals with interaction of people, and the *process* center automatically responds with well-learned behaviors to present circumstances.

Motives are learned through repetitive actions that eventually become more a part of the *process* center. However, if the *process* center is predominantly engaged during an assessment, then what is being assessed is the picture itself, and not assessing and reflecting on the relationships and activities of the people in the picture. The latter assessments can potentially project motives of the respondent. Motives are inherently human and the *social* center needs to be engaged in the assessment. Respondents are asked to think about what the other people are thinking, and as a result are putting themselves in their shoes, thus projecting their own motives. By presenting a neutral prompt like a picture of people, the respondent, when given the freedom of writing a story, issues forth a human-oriented response from the *social* center. Thus, the story assessment elicits a natural human-oriented response that represents human interests or motives.

An MBTI-brain functioning study was conducted to see if a person uses different parts of their brain when answering the simple questions on the MBTI® assessment. The idea was to see if a personality type showed differing brain activity. Probes were attached to every significant part of the brain with activity in these parts recorded during testing. What was revealed was a tendency to actually use different parts of the brain in the three concepts of *introvert/extrovert*, *thinking/feeling*, and *judging/perceiving*, as subjects tested for these using the simple question-answer test. However, *sensing/intuitive* did not yield a distinction between them. With the *sensing/intuitive* distinction the person is expected to look for detail in *sensing*, but see the big picture in *intuitive*. The simple questions are about what you think (detail), not what you would intuit, hence the *intuition* questions are actually *sensing* questions. Since the assessment itself is a problem to be resolved, the brain uses the *executive* center and not the *social* center. The social center could, in fact, interpret something more inclusive than just the question itself, such as reactions to pictures of people engaged in an activity. But the simple questions do not elicit that. Each simple question was unintendedly a *sensing* question and not one that would reveal a wider *intuitive* response. To assess the *sensing/intuitive* distinction you would answer the *sensing* question: "Do you like working with detail?"; and with the same brain activity as the *intuitive* question "Do you enjoy seeing the big picture?" Question-answer cognitive assessments cannot prompt the more natural personal response, but reveal only what one <u>thinks</u> about themselves. While what one thinks about themselves is useful information, it falls short of revealing a complete personal picture. Natural motives assessment provides something different from simple question-answer testing.

Learning Growth and Training of Motives

Have you ever noticed how some dogs pay very close attention to their owners when they are being taken for a walk, while other dogs pull and yank on their leashes? It is almost as if these ill-behaved dogs are taking their owners for a walk. Most well-behaved dogs have learned to walk gently with their owners because they have been taught to do so, normally by reinforced learning. The learned behavior is reinforced by an incentive to act a certain way, perhaps with a doggie treat. Any ordinary dog can learn with proper reinforcements/incentives. Reinforcement/incentive learning also can explain how some motive learning occurs for the ordinary person.

Learning takes place in many circumstances of life that sometimes produce amazing results. Tiger Woods, one of the great golfers of all time, most likely never would have become a star in what has become one of the world's most popular sports. The sport's popularity, and thus Tiger Wood's celebrity status, can be attributed to a former great golfer, Arnold Palmer. The popularity of golf accelerated once Palmer started winning and became respectful and personally engaged with those that followed his play. He became so popular that the people who followed him began to be known as Arnie's Army. Some would even say that Arnold Palmer saved professional golf, and gave subsequent professional golfers, such as Tiger Woods, a stage to launch great careers. Arnold Palmer is a good example about how motives can be learned, resulting in making an amazing difference. What is fascinating is not HOW Arnold Palmer learned to play golf, but WHY he learned (his motives). Palmer's story starts with his father leaving an indoor job to take a job as a ditch digger for a new golf course being constructed. His father stayed on and eventually became the head greenskeeper, learning as he went, and then became head golf pro. He began taking his son Arnold with him to work. Arnold wanted to be with his father and share his interest and became enamored with the game of golf. He started learning the game because of his desire to be with his father, a disciplinarian, who ensured Arnold would learn the game well. Of course, the end result of this story is that Arnold Palmer made golf popular for so many because of his graciousness and thoughts of fair play. For him it was not just about golf, but about people, his father being one, who sparked his growing interest in the game itself. In his later years Arnold Palmer commented:

> "The people I have met have made
> my life special. If you're a golfer

reading this, think about how many people you've met and made friends with because you played golf. Then take another person who doesn't play golf I don't care where you are or what sport you're in, it can't compare, in my mind, to golf in bringing people together. Golf is a world in itself. It's an experience that's really worth living. It's been a wonderful life, I must say, and I say so with all humility and with appreciation for the people who made it so special."

The positive feedback, or incentive for Arnold Palmer, was his success at golf. Yet that success was energized by social relationships, his need to be with people and count them as friends, while living a life filled with respecting and honoring relationships. His natural motives were *affiliation* and *personal causation*. Later when he became more *achievement* oriented, he began to win, thus, reinforcing his personal motives of *achievement, affiliation,* and *personal causation*. (As an interesting note, Tiger Woods was also introduced to golf by his father.)

Another example of motives being learned is Eleanor Roosevelt. Her background was much different from Arnold Palmer. She was born into high society with an uncle who was president, a socialite mother who died early, and father who was mostly absent due to addictions. With an education from various places, she was taught to reach out on her own, to set personal goals, and to be aware of the effect of her behavior on others. Her success came as first lady, in acting as the legs and often the goodwill ambassador for President Franklin Roosevelt. She led many benevolent and worthy causes, and published across various disciplines successfully. She looked for the creative experiences of life along with what they meant within their circumstances. She wrote "... to know what you see and to understand what it means..." Also, her view of a personal life was to be filled with "curiosity, interest, imagination, and a sense of adventure of life." Her natural motives were *personal causation*, *power* (with others in mind), and *achievement*. Her motives were unlike Arnold Palmer's motives but she was successful, as he was, in her life's pursuits because she found ways to engage her motives.

Acquiring Motives

Motives are learned over time through a combination of opportunities presenting themselves, also called demands from the environment, matched up with incentives that initiate, build, and reinforce a particular motive. People not only learn skills from repetition, but preferences for behavior when the behavior is reinforced by an incentive. If after a long day's work, you may personally find it an incentive to receive a pat on the back from the boss, which reinforces the *achievement* motive of a hard day's work. After a series of actions and reinforcements of the same motive, the motive turns out to be part of a person's normal way of acting and becomes a disposition or trait. There is a deep tendency or interest to behave in a motivated way when a motive has been learned and an opportunity presents itself that engages that motive disposition/trait. Arnold Palmer, having learned that golf can be associated with social or friendship feelings, was drawn to golf as a natural behavior from his *affiliative* motive, not something that must be done to become rich and famous. Eleanor Roosevelt, with her motive of *personal causation*, chose to act independently and not just abide by predefined roles.

Opportunities or demands from the environment can make a difference in behavior when encountered and undertaken. Motives are learned when there is an incentive that produces a positive result within the individual. Incentives are personal, and range across many forms. For instance, how an individual is comfortable in their world with variety, where variety is represented by familiarity-novelty, expectedness–surprising, clarity–ambiguity, complexity–simplicity. Also, individuals are comfortable with a certain level of impact such as producing effects in the environment versus conformity as in personal self-consistency and/or social expectations. They also have expectations in a certain level of consistency in personal values. Motive dispositions are a recurrent concern over a goal state that drives, orients, and selects behavior. An aroused motive is satisfying a motive disposition that has been activated by opportunities or demands. See Figure 2-4.

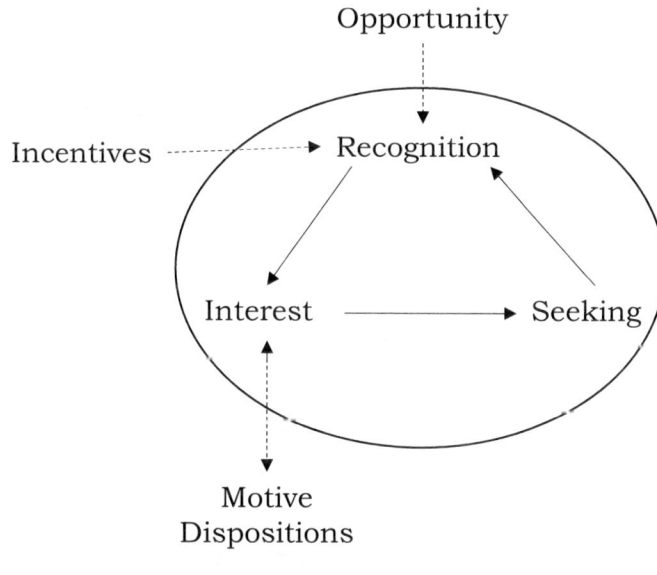

Figure 2-4
Learning Motives

Learning and arousing/activating the motive process is somewhat circular. A motive is learned when the opportunity and incentive are recognized by the person thus building an interest and a motive disposition. Often opportunities present themselves after a motive has been learned where these opportunities engage a motive disposition arousing the motive leading to motivated behavior, or behavior that comes naturally from the interests one has acquired. The learning process short circuits the need for recognition and interest which results in the opportunity producing motivated behavior itself.

Motives in Your Life

John Grisham, a famous author, has written nearly fifty books. His writing career is echoed in history with other prolific writers such as Ian Fleming, writer of the James Bond collection; Rex Stout creator of the Nero Wolf collection; and Erle Stanley Gardner, author of many volumes about the famous fictional lawyer, Perry Mason. What could motivate such writing behavior? For example, Gardner spent hours every day writing. When he arose at dawn and saw the sun, and upon entering his study, this circumstance became a cue or demand that aroused his already learned motives of *personal causation* and *achievement* which led to his writing. While his motives were what really interested him, it was the cue of entering his study that produced the behavior which satisfied his learned motives. Even when a motive is aroused, it does not necessarily produce a behavior. We often consider our behavior before acting, that is, we can think before we act. However, on many occasions we engage in behavior that is naturally motivated, through an aroused motive, entering into a flow state. A flow state is one where activities engaged in produce a feeling of self-fulfillment. Hobbies often produce a flow state, where one starts living in this natural state. It is often so natural that one loses track of time. Perhaps you have heard statements as "When Frank gets in his workshop, he does not know what time it is." "When Jan goes shopping you never know when to meet her afterwards." "Not sure when Pat will be home from work, that job just seems to eat up the time." By the way, Gardner put a timeframe on his writing. He wrote, or often dictated, his stories from dawn until breakfast, then he would quit to eat. This forced stop solved the problem of getting too caught up in the writing, a flow state. See Figure 2-5.

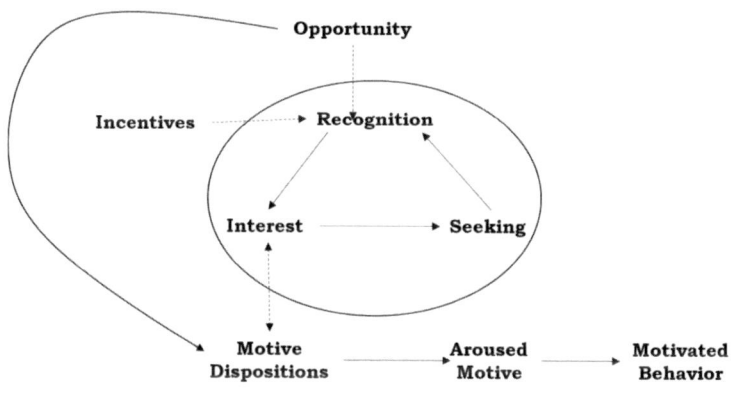

Figure 2-5
Motivated Behavior

Mastery Approach to Motives Growth

Motives can be learned or grown over time using a mastery approach. My personal experiences have taught me a great deal about mastery learning. While in the first part of a four-year career in the air force my goal was to get through basic electronics training without over-exerting myself. As a young man there were plenty of things to do other than spend a lot of mental, emotional, or physical energy in electronics training. I thought to myself "Do my time and get on with the next assignment." This was both socially acceptable to my buddies, and really matched my well-developed skill for avoiding work-related activities. Then it happened. I flunked one set in the series that was required. An officer responsible for training the troops counseled me in ways Mom may have found offensive. They assigned me to the slower learning group and offered me the "option" of study hall, get it in gear or I'd be cooking (read pulling permanent KP) in Vietnam. This was 1966. Okay, that goal of just getting through was not going to work. This was what has been described as a triggering event or paradigm shift – something that initiated a whole new viewpoint. Being unsure of what the new goal should be, I devoted myself to learning. I earned commendations in each of the remaining sets of training classes. This set me on a new path. One of my mentors along this path related to me that it is not how smart you are but how persistently hard you try.

The message gained from my experience is that goals become secondary considerations because once you decide on a journey, the journey becomes primary. This was my initiation to a road of mastery for learning that stayed with me throughout my air force and university careers. Without it, I may have ended up flipping hamburgers -- although being a master chef is a worthy pursuit. Triggering events do not always have to be failures but they often are and cause serious soul searching. Failure of a project or group of projects may bring on defensive reasoning, which concentrates on defending the failure rather than seeking the reasons for it. If one is looking for the reasons of a failure a new path can then be initiated.

Mastery is a path not a goal. It is a step function where each step or plateau provides opportunities to practice, and eventually be rewarded with a higher level of what is being learned. Mastery requires a tolerance for delayed gratification. The steps of practice are repetitive, not immediately rewarding, and not equally accomplished within the same timeframe for every individual. The flat zone between growth areas on the path of mastery can make one feel they have regressed but in actuality they are preparing for the next leap. See Figure 2-6.

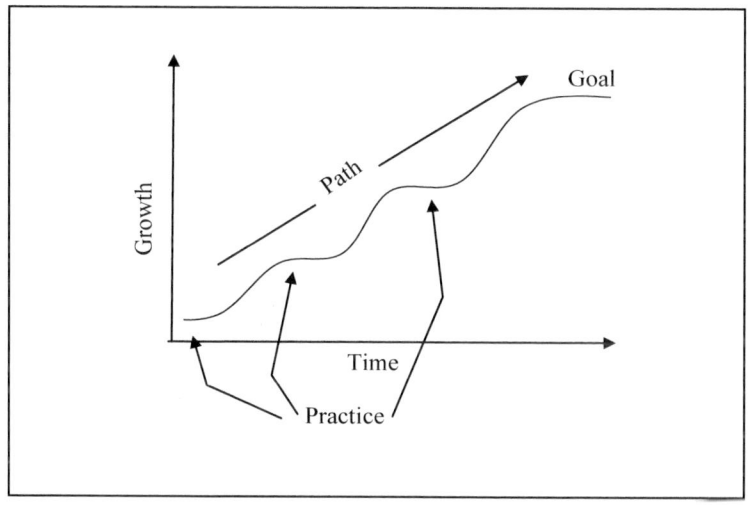

Figure 2-6
Mastery Process

Mastering anything requires commitment, specifically, get on the path and do not simply decide on the goals. It requires dedication, namely practicing within levels for as long as it takes to reach new plateaus. And it requires surrendering the thinking that good enough is not good enough. George Leonard, in his little book on *Mastery,* outlines five keys.

1. Instruction: You need a teacher

2. Practice: Something separated from the rest of your life

3. Surrender: To your teacher, to the discipline, away from personal dignity

4. Intentionality: See a vision of what is to be accomplished (the goal)

5. Edge: Test the edges in search of a larger/greater outcome

Mastering takes a commitment to a long-term goal. When you think you know more than the teacher, you are off the path; when you think practice will not substantially improve your performance, you are off the path; when you think there are many other things of higher priority in your life then you are off the path; when you think about the end goal without much specificity, you are off the path; and, when you think you have done this long enough to really be good you've lost the edge and you are off the path. Mastery is more about character and building character than it is about recognition of performance. With character it is possible to achieve a mastery path, without it we are actors without a role to play. As one great leader, coach, and mentor John Wooden said: "Be more concerned with your character than your reputation, because your character is what you really are, while your reputation is merely what others think you are."

Growing a motive can be thought of as a mastery approach. For each motive, improvements are possible resulting in behavioral choices that can be very meaningful, namely, a new job, new or better relationships, or starting or renewing a hobby. Two things are needed to grow a motive: one is to know what the motive is in general and two is to have the motive exemplified through actions of others and reflective personal life experiences. Sometimes without the aid of others a natural path to motive growth may be missed. We are often satisfied with what we have learned in terms of our motives, but the degree of learning is not always evident to the individual.

To facilitate this "experiential" learning a coach or mentor can prove to be very valuable. Qualities of an effective coach are listed below.

1. Know personal desires/wishes/preferences
2. Establish a motive reality focus (cognitive and natural)
3. Assist in setting natural behavioral goals with empathy
4. Provide feedback to encourage natural behaviors
5. Be appropriately social

Motives Training

Each of the four motives, *achievement, affiliation, power,* and *personal causation* can be increased through formal training. Training for each of these motives has been conducted in a classroom setting requiring the participants to be open to learning. There have been before-and-after motive measures in each of these training experiences which demonstrate their effectiveness. While the circumstances of the training are different these instances show the malleability of motives.

Each training experience involved learning the motive along with activities that provided personal experiences of it. One result of this sort of training is to be able to engage the five keys of mastery (see above) in order to be on a mastery track for a motive. Several elements are used as an overall model for each motive training session. These elements are:

1. Know the motive through its definition and descriptions (knowledge)
2. Be able to recognize and score the motive in stories written by others (recognition)
3. Work through exercises that target the motive usage (personal experience)
4. Testimonial of people with a high degree of the motive (encouragement)

5. Personal description of what to do to increase the motive (commitment)

Mentors and coaches can help suggest training and provide a level of inspiration to keep commitments.

One *achievement* motive training was conducted with a group of business associates in a small city in India to improve business activity. As a controlled study the details showed that those attending the training improved the business climate for their city. Results were compared with another similar city in India that served as a comparison for judging the change. The training involved learning the *achievement* motive in detail (knowledge); scoring *achievement* stories (recognition); participating in exercises that engaged *achievement* through goal setting activities (personal experience); and testimonials by people who have achieved great things in their lives (encouragement). Participants were also expected to write strategy statements about how they will enhance their *achievement* motive (commitment). (See Appendix 2 for examples of commitment.)

An instance of *affiliation* training involved a class which divided into teams, to learn how to conduct one-on-one meetings within each team, and how to score each other on their personal effectiveness. This built their confidence for personal interaction and evidenced how being friendly and helping others can lead to a positive outcome (personal experience). They were taught the details of the *affiliation* motive through classroom presentations and examples (knowledge). They were also expected to write strategies about how they will interact with others better (commitment).

The *power* motive was taught to managers of sales people by training the managers to understand the motive (knowledge); to learn how to score stories for *power* (recognition); to conduct reviews of case studies to exemplify how *power* can be a positive characteristic (encouragement); and to perform exercises that required the usage of personal control for the good of the others (personal experience). Results showed not only a more positive impression of their overall business climate, but an increase in actual sales.

The *personal causation* motive was taught (knowledge) to teachers in selected grade schools so they could create in their students a sense of personal initiation of responsible activity. Scoring stories was used (recognition) with examples of a low versus a high degree of *personal causation*; and they conducted exercises that had learners experience both low and high *personal causation* (personal experience). Results showed that students in classrooms where teachers were taught *personal causation* were much more successful in future classes over students in classrooms where teachers were not trained in *personal causation*.

Motives are acquired in two ways; in one they are garnered through life experiences and, in another, they are gained through organized classroom programs. Motives are learned, grown, and many times revealed by natural motive assessments and effective coaching. The motives of a*chievement, affiliation, power,* and *personal causation* are foundational to understanding and engaging in motivated behavior. These motives are discovered by assessments and grown and learned through special training, and selective life experiences.

Motives in Your Life

Chapter 3

Motives and Leadership

The miracle, or the power, that elevates the few is to be found in their perseverance under the promptings of a brave, determined spirit.

Mark Twain

Simply stated the key to leadership is motivation. Through the efforts of others and your own inherent and acquired energy, leadership emerges. Not only should a leader be able to realize the application of their motives, but should understand how and what motivates others. Above all else a leader's core interests are the force which drives motivation.

In this chapter these interests are examined along with three leadership notions and how they apply to these notions. The three dimensions are leadership in an organizational culture (i.e., "The organization where I work") leadership as a concept/philosophy (i.e., "My personal idea of leadership"); and leadership as a role needed within various circumstances (i.e., "The elements of the job to be done"). There is a Behavior Potential associated with each of these dimensions. By examining leadership through these three dimensions each dimension's Behavior Potential is revealed; that is when you look at leadership within a certain dimension, possible actions are more evident. The examination of the motivational elements of leadership dimensions with one's personal and leadership motives syndromes can result in an understanding and the development of a natural form of leadership.

Leadership naturally emerges from relationships among people within an environment or situation. Circumstances range from personal, with family and friends, to professional within various businesses and benevolent enterprises. No matter the scenario leadership is a concept understood as a special status held by a person or people within a situation.

Leadership certainly has been given a lot of attention. One popular publication website lists over 60,000 leadership book titles. Definitions aside, what we find here is leadership plays a role in almost anything, in organizations, in nursing, and even in gardening. Also, leadership exists within the overall concept of service leadership, tribal leadership, graceful leadership, emotional leadership, and others. However, leadership from a personal interest perspective is the main concern because what interests an individual is that which motivates them most successfully. Motives are the basis for natural leadership for an individual. When the situation engages a particular kind of interest, as expressed through motive syndromes, you may find yourself a natural for it.

Motives - Leadership Syndromes

One's personal interests can align with the requirements for leadership. When this happens more effective leadership can result, along with a level of personal satisfaction. We are most engaged with activities we find interesting which seem to carry us forward; these are the things that motivate us. Natural motives are key. We find acting on them to be internally satisfying and relevant to our way of doing things. Motives that emphasize control and how that control is applied within settings creates a personal interest in leading. Both *power* and *personal causation* motives provide control and the internal energy for someone to act. This energy is then applied to accomplishing something, satisfying the *achievement* motive; or to creating and sustaining relationships, satisfying the *affiliation* motive. Four leadership motive syndromes result when combining these motives. First, the *Influencer* syndrome combines the *power* motive with the *affiliation* motive. Second, the *Mover* syndrome merges the *power* motive with the *achievement* motive. Third, the I*nnovator* syndrome unites the *personal causation* motive with the *achievement* motive. And, lastly, the fourth, the *Ambassador* syndrome combines the *personal causation* motive with the *affiliation* motive. The more generalized terms used in personality syndromes of *Persuader, Initiator, Doer,* and *Overcomer* match up with the leadership syndromes of *Influencer, Ambassador, Mover,* and *Innovator* respectively. Using different motive syndrome descriptors for leadership versus personality simply provide a better understanding of leadership versus personality. Personality descriptors apply to any behavioral opportunities, while leadership descriptors apply to leadership situations. The personality generalized syndrome descriptors are used throughout the book to provide a common thread across the application of motives for other areas. (See Figure 3-1). Characteristics of the leadership motive syndromes are shown in Figure 3-2.

Applied Motives

		Achievement	*Affiliation*
	Power	*Mover* Leader *Doer* Personality	*Influencer* Leader *Persuader* Personality
Control Motives	*Personal Causation*	*Innovator* Leader *Overcomer* Personality	*Ambassador* Leader *Initiator* Personality

Leadership Motive Syndromes
Figure 3-1

Mover Leader	Influencer Leader
Doer	**Persuader**
Achievement Seek out and do better at moderately difficult tasks Take personal responsibility for performance Seek performance feedback Try new and more efficient ways	Affiliation Establishing relationships Maintaining relationships Restoring relationships Caring for others Sensitive to needs
Power Having impact on another Influence others Having impact on the world at large Gaining or limiting prestige	Power Having impact on another Influence others Having impact on the world at large Gaining or limiting prestige
M. Thatcher	D.D. Eisenhower

Innovator Leader	Ambassador Leader
Overcomer	**Initiator**
Achievement Seek out and do better at moderately difficult tasks Take personal responsibility for performance Seek performance feedback Try new and more efficient ways	Affiliation Establishing relationships Maintaining relationships Restoring relationships Caring for others Sensitive to needs
Personal Causation Originating behavior Sees reality of goals Sees personal responsibility Anticipates outcome	Personal Causation Originating behavior Sees reality of goals Sees personal responsibility Anticipates outcome
Steve Jobs	St Teresa

Characteristics of Leadership with Motive Syndromes
Figure 3-2

Motives in Your Life

Dwight D. Eisenhower, the 34th President of the United States, exemplifies the *Influencer* leader syndrome. He had primary motives of *power* and *affiliation*. Since his family was of modest income, he and his brother made a pact in which each year one would attend college while the other worked to pay the tuition on an alternating basis. Later he learned that he might be able to attend a military academy tuition free, so he applied to the Naval Academy and West Point and was accepted by both. However, he had become too old for the Naval Academy so he enrolled in West Point. Dwight graduated in the middle of his class at West Point where he was a good athlete and socially active, but did not focus on his studies. The fact that he was a student of military history at an early age and had a West Point education certainly made a difference in his career. He evolved into the "go to" guy for strategic planning, often known as the person who brought people together to take action. In planning the invasion of Europe during World War Two and in gathering major leaders throughout the free world to collaborate, he accomplished a great feat. He understood power for its impact on people, and how to manage relationships for the ultimate good – key characteristics of an *Influencer* leader syndrome.

Margaret Thatcher, the "Iron Lady" of British politics, is a good example of a *Mover* leader syndrome. As was stated in the New York Times:

> ...set her country on a rightward economic course, led it to victory in the Falklands War and helped guide the United States and the Soviet Union through the Cold War's difficult last years...by the time she left office, the principles known as Thatcherism — the belief that economic freedom and individual liberty are interdependent, that personal responsibility and hard work are the only ways to national prosperity, and that the free-market

democracies must stand firm against aggression — had won many disciples. Even some of her strongest critics accorded her a grudging respect.

She changed the economic and social atmosphere through her sense of power for the good of the people with an energy toward accomplishment. She combined the motives of *power* and *achievement* to lead a nation during the difficulties of the Cold War and much unrest in the nation itself. Although some of her accomplishments are viewed as contrary to the overall good, results of her actions were remarkable and show the impact of a great *Mover* leader syndrome.

Steve Jobs is an example of the *Innovator* leader syndrome. His creative energy initiated a variety of Apple products and their subsequent success to achieve one of the greatest product accomplishments of the century. He made a difference through personal energy and was the driving force who brought about a communications cultural change for most of the world. Not only did he create product, but he led Apple from the brink of bankruptcy when he returned to the company after other creative endeavors. His creative personality can be summed up with his own admonition "Stay Hungry. Stay Foolish." He epitomizes someone with great personal energy along with someone who is driven to achieve. His innate desire for accomplishment can be sensed in his pitch to Mr. Sculley, a former Pepsi-Cola chief executive to be Apple's chief executive: "Do you want to spend the rest of your life selling sugared water, or do you want a chance to change the world?" Steve Jobs's energy sprouted or grew from his *personal causation* motive, and his desire to accomplish from his *achievement* motive – a great example of an *Innovator* leader syndrome.

Saint Teresa of Calcutta was a Roman Catholic nun and missionary teacher at the Loreto convent school in Entally, eastern Calcutta. She is a good example of the *Ambassador* leader syndrome. She served twenty years at the school and was appointed its headmistress. Increasingly disturbed by the poverty, famine, misery, and death surrounding her in Calcutta, she felt she should serve the poor by staying with them. She left the school and founded the 'Missionaries of Charity.' Teresa adopted Indian citizenship and ventured into the slums after months in basic medical training. The mission still manages homes for people who are dying of HIV/AIDS, leprosy and tuberculosis. It runs soup kitchens, dispensaries, mobile clinics, children and family counseling programs, orphanages and schools. Those that serve in the mission take vows of chastity, poverty, and obedience while giving "wholehearted free service to the poorest of the poor." Mother Teresa put together her deep desire for people with an energy that drove her personally to make a difference. The Sisters of Charity mission is "...the hungry, the naked, the homeless, the crippled, the blind, the lepers, all those people who feel unwanted, unloved, uncared for throughout society, people that have become a burden to the society and are shunned by everyone." Her *affiliation* motive coupled with her *personal causation* motive provide us with a prime example of the *Ambassador* leader syndrome. When engaging personal interest, as indicated by motives, the job of leading becomes natural and self-fulfilling.

Leadership characteristics can reveal one's suitability to lead within various leadership states. These instances include one's personal leadership philosophy; the demands presented by individual circumstances; and overall expectations from an environment or culture of a business enterprise, namely, its organizational culture.

Dimension 1 - Organizational Culture Leadership

The organization where I work

Leading others is a social engagement which, in turn, demands certain social statuses and practices that have become the norm. In the business sense, the overall social environment is known as the organizational culture of the company. In brief, organizational culture is "the way we do things around here," and it is usually off-conscious, that is, people cannot describe their organizational culture since they have become part of it. It would be a bit like asking a flower to describe itself since its identity is itself. One cannot step away from one's identity and then describe it. Effective leadership is a builder of culture plus shaped by culture. Four organizational cultures are identified on two axes: the amount of control exerted as either strong or weak, and the focus of attention as either internal or external to the organization. These, in turn, can be associated with leadership syndromes. The four organizational cultures are *target* with its high level of control and external focus, *ordered* with high level of control and internal focus, *entrepreneurial* with low level of control and external focus, and *familial/clan* with its low level of control and internal focus.

Leadership requires a measure of social control while considering what behavior is acceptable within the organizational culture itself. For example, in organizing a family picnic, which is a *familial/clan* culture, it is primarily important to ensure people support the experience with a concern for relationships. However, if the leadership responsibility is to feed students in a cafeteria by having the meal start and end on time with efficient use of food (a worthy "lunch" goal achievement); achieving the goal is more important than consideration for the relationships of the students. One way to consider culture is to determine if there is a high level of control or not, as well as whether its focus is internal or external. In both the examples above, there is an internal focus, but with the picnic, the control is less than in the cafeteria example.

Business examples of these cultures can provide additional insights. A high level of control with an internal focus is an *ordered* culture and one company that has this culture is U.S. Steel. Alternately, a low level of control with an internal focus is a *familial/clan* culture, as would be the case with Chick-fil-A or Nike. A high level of control with an external focus is a *target* culture. Many large business enterprises such as Amazon are *target* cultures. A low level of control with an external focus is an *entrepreneurial* culture, such as, most major sports enterprises as the St Louis Cardinals or Facebook, the social media company. Each of these cultures can best be served by leaders who have a particular leadership syndrome, that is, a set of motives consistent with the rules or mores of the culture.

Leaders function within cultures. When a leader has a certain set of motives, then he/she may find it more fulfilling to lead in one organizational culture over another. Leaders who are high in the *power* motive are more comfortable in a culture that requires more control, while leaders high in *personal causation* motive have some control but concentrate more on personal freedom and influence. Leaders high in the *affiliation* motive are concerned with having an impact on relationships, while those high in the *achievement* motive are more attuned to reaching particular goals. The four motive syndromes align with the four organizational cultures. An *ordered* culture with its high level of control and internal focus is best served by the *Influencer* leader. They are most comfortable having an impact, not on just reaching an outcome, but predominantly on how relationships among and between people are managed. A *target* culture with its high control requirement and external focus would best be served by a *Mover* leader. In an *entrepreneurial* culture with more personal control and external focus, a leader with high *personal causation* motive along with high *achievement* motive is identified as an *Innovator* leader. Lastly, in a *familial/clan* culture with more personal control needed for an internal focus, someone with a high *personal causation* and high *affiliation* motives would be most comfortable in a leadership position, thus, identified as an *Ambassador* leader. See Figure 3-3.

Organizational culture leadership presents challenges within a variety of fluid and subjective contexts. Also, it is important to recognize that leadership, when it is contra-cultural, may be successful yet cause strain and duress. So, gaging social control levels is necessary and determining what is acceptable in an organizational culture are factors to consider as you move forward.

Culture Focus

		External	Internal
		Achievement	*Affiliation*
High	*Power*	*Mover* Leader (Margaret Thatcher) TARGET culture (Amazon)	*Influencer* Leader (Dwight D. Eisenhower) ORDERED Culture (U.S. Steel)
Lower	*Personal Causation*	*Innovation* Leader (Steve Jobs) ENTREPRENEURIAL Culture (Facebook)	*Ambassador* Leader (Mother Teresa) FAMILIAL/CLAN Culture (Chick-fil-A)

Culture Control (vertical axis label)

Figure 3-3
Culture and Leadership Syndromes

If you are in an organizational culture that is compatible with your leadership syndrome you have the opportunity to be a natural leader. If there is no compatibility, then it is helpful to recognize this and make changes either by changing organizational cultures, educating yourself on the motives needed (see Appendix 3), or realizing you must use various ways to cope with the situation. In any large organization you can usually find a variety of cultures, and finding the one that best fits your motives may be worth the time and energy.

Activities in these various cultures would be carried out in different ways. For instance, meetings in a *target* culture usually would be accompanied by a preset agenda with a consideration on how the organization's goals fit the agenda. In an *entrepreneurial* culture the meetings would have open agendas and considerable attention would be given to a plan of action for the near future. Meetings in the *ordered* culture would have set agendas with pre-discussions on what the agenda should contain. These meetings would also conclude with a set of actions that would need to be taken soon after the meeting. Detailed planning in these organizations is usually given much attention. In the familial/clan culture meetings limited, unstructured agenda items would be the norm. Also, there would be discussions before and after the meeting to interpret what next steps to take, what activities might be suitable later, and what the impact of the meeting was on everyone who participated. Planning takes on a different form in the sense that it is not so much activities in a plan but the value of the plan to the individuals who participate in the fulfillment of it.

Dimension 2 - Leadership Philosophy

My personal idea of leadership

While organizational culture sets the social stage for expected leadership techniques or methods, each person has his own concept of leadership independent of environmental influences. In acquiring a personal concept or definition of leadership, we may produce within ourselves a leadership philosophy. This is something we hold deeply by recognizing it in others and in ourselves. It is a personal trait that is consistent across time and situations. However, differences in leadership philosophies can be observed across situations.

Let us assume you enter the office and you overhear two co-workers in a heated discussion about which area should respond to a technical problem, thereby disrupting others and their work. As a leader in the situation, you pop your head into the cubicle and ask them to come to your office. There you learn that each person is not really emotionally distraught, but their loud interaction is simply the way they choose to communicate. You suggest in the future they use a conference room to reduce disturbance of others, and commend them for their concern about addressing the technical problem. As an effective leader, you assume that your private discussion with them will help their behavior.

To illustrate further, your boss storms into your office the next day and in a loud voice, informs you that you have failed to correctly prioritize a project that is critical to the company. He requests that you report back to him next week on how you have fixed the priority problem. He adds that mistakes are inevitable, then marches out. He is assuming a good leader is somewhat "all knowing" and has a clear path to lead, and those who follow need to conform to it.

In another example, one day your boss's boss comes into your office and asks if you would make a presentation to the board of directors for the first time. She will review it with you, but indicates that you know more about the specifics than anyone else including her. Her leadership assumption is that the follower can make significant contributions, and can be depended upon to represent her to others. This is quite unlike your boss who assumes you have little, if nothing, to contribute to a decision or interaction.

In another case your brother comes home on leave from the Marines. During a complaining session about his commander, the commander calls and requests your brother return, thus, cutting his leave short. Your brother immediately begins to pack. You are confused and comment, "I thought you really disliked him as a leader." "I do, but he has the office, and I need to respect the office." It does not matter if the commander believes he is right, or if he should interact with a subordinate to get their input, his position is what counts.

Each highlighted individual in these examples has a leadership philosophy. We observed that these are based on the assumption that leadership can be within a person, as your boss believes by issuing his directions, or could be outside a person, as with your boss's boss who leads by seeking outside interaction from you, or in an official designation as with your brother who assumes leadership is in the position or rank no matter who holds it. A personal leadership philosophy is assumed to be within a person, outside a person, or in a formal social role.

With the assumption that an individual possesses leadership, it could be assumed to be an identity from birth, or alternately, that it matures within the individual over time. The *born* predominate leadership philosophy can be characterized as the "I am" leadership position. Leadership capability appears at birth and experiences provide opportunity for this natural capability to be realized. For a *maturing* leadership philosophy, the leadership quality of the "self" is assumed to be developmental, and it can be characterized as "I've become" a leader. If the leadership position is assumed to be outside the person, then leadership needs to be granted or given by someone in power, or given by others in the environment.

If someone in power *selects* you as leader, it is an "I'm appointed" approach. If leadership can be *earned* from others, it is the "I'm confirmed" as a leader approach. Leadership can be assumed to come from a place where the person is within a given organizational structure. The place can be a *formal* identification where leadership is in a rank and not necessarily the person. In a military example, one is promoted from Captain to Major and with that promotion may come additional leadership expectations. This is the "I hold" approach at leadership. Also, it can be assumed a person has leadership from outside, as in a *social* place. The social order recognizes someone as very special as in healer/medicine man. One attains the position through a collection of social mores and acts. It is the "I'm recognized" idea of leadership. (See Figures 3-4 and 3-5.)

In summary, this has examined leadership philosophies through a study of personal leadership concepts and assumptions.

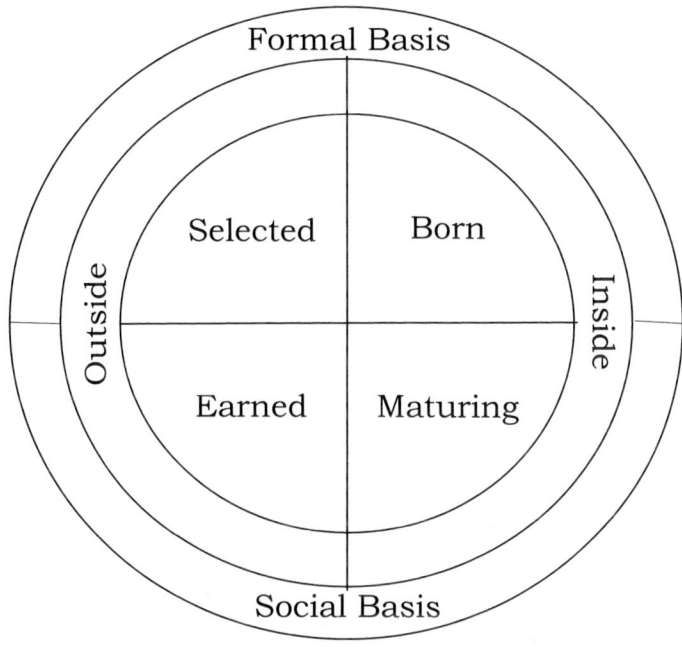

Figure 3-4
Leadership Philosophies

	Leader	Description
Basis	Formal	"I hold" leadership position is similar to the "I'm appointed" leader. The exception is office of leader, perhaps designed by a rank or title as in "the president" where the office itself deserves leadership by implied honor.
	Social	"I'm recognized" leader is identified closely with the community of followers. Few people question the leader's role as someone who understands things the followers do not and, hence, are relied upon to offer advice as opinion leaders.
Application	Born	"I am" notion of leadership is a trait that comes from birth and is realized during maturity. Experiences have little to do with the trait other than expose it to the light. Leadership behavior is engrained and only to be released.
	Maturing	"I've become" leader is recognition that leadership is learned. By assessing who others are and who one is in relationship to them, it is possible to guide them into performance and achievements.
	Selected	"I'm appointed" leadership position is where the leader is given the role by someone in power. Others are expected to follow because they have been designated to do explicitly or implicitly.
	Earned	"I'm confirmed" leader comes from an extrinsic recognition by followers that this person is a leader. Followers give credit to the leader because they are aware of the leader's capability and assign their allegiance.

Figure 3-5

Descriptions of Leadership Philosophies

It is important that the individual recognizes his personal leadership philosophy whether leading, being led, or engaging with other leaders. The well documented Shackleton expedition to the Antarctic on the ship *Endurance* provides a clear example of how leadership philosophy can have a powerful effect on behavior. The expedition itself was a failure in that it did not reach the initial goal, yet in a critical way it was a success – the crew should have died but were all saved through heroic efforts. The *Endurance* became stranded in ice packed waters, and the crew had to abandon ship hundreds of miles from any land mass. The crew all lived with the assumption that Expedition Head Ernest Shackleton and Captain Frank Worsley were to always be leaders of the expedition due to their formal positions. When the ship had to be abandoned, one man decided Shackleton and Worsley were no longer the leaders because the circumstances had changed, namely, they were no longer on the ship. Yet the crew did not mutiny but stuck to the formal tradition of the captain as leader. The one man who wanted to mutiny felt that leadership was a social role that needed to be earned, and not assumed to be present upon a formal appointment. Due to limited resources, a harsh deadly environment, and few options, a formal leadership approach was required. There was no time for negotiation using the give and take a social leadership approach needs. Due to the acceptance of a formal leadership philosophy by the crew, they were able to be led to overcome great odds, stay optimistic about their chances, and survive the journey. If the crew had decided to re-think their leadership philosophy, or come to recognize a different philosophy other than a formal one, they would have likely perished.

Problems can happen when you have a personal philosophy that is not compatible with the reality of the circumstance. Imagine that you are an "appointed" leader as in the *selected* philosophy where someone has assigned you to that role. However, your own leadership philosophy is *earned* and you expect to become the leader, not by mere assignments, but by being effective through engaging with your followers. Even though you may hold the *selected* position of leader, in your own mind, you will not be effective until your leadership is *earned* from your followers. If there is no time, as in the Shackleton expedition, then your personal leadership philosophy will lead to failure if followed. Circumstances most often dictate the most effective leadership to employ even though it may not reflect the personal philosophy of the leader. Personal leadership philosophies may need to be overlooked to be effective in such circumstances. Let us assume Joe is "confirmed" by his followers as leader but does not feel he is a real leader until he is assigned the *formal* place of leadership. While waiting for an official assignment, his followers flounder due to his assumed lack of leadership. Many leadership failures can be attributed to a leader waiting to be given the role through selection, thus, lacking the time to mature into it, or not be given the opportunity to earn it from the followers. One must avoid leading according to your own personal philosophy in all circumstances. Anyone may potentially be an effective leader even when circumstances work against a personal philosophy, providing they can recognize their own philosophy and how circumstances demand a different direction. Knowing one's personal philosophy of leadership can help bring about effective leadership when the leader recognizes it and knows what is really needed.

Some people have a predominant leadership philosophy and others have a mixture with no predominant one. A predominant leadership philosophy can be identified by specific behaviors and how to engage with them, as shown in Figure 3-6.

Leader		How to Identify	How to Engage	Other Issues
Basis	Formal	Gives orders Confident Impersonal, aloof Trustworthy Hidden intentions	Integrity Fulfill trust Allegiance, Obedience Respect Confirm assignment	Clear, well-defined channels of communicati on that are to be used
	Social	Wise Generate new ideas Translates Knows the ropes	Interpretation Favors Honor Know history	Needs a social order that comes through a history of interactions
Application	Born	Ego driven Commanding Solution oriented Opportunity seeker Focused	Confidence Fact-based questions Encourage positive spin You are an opportunity	Demonstrate ability by using staff effectively
	Maturing	Flexible Inquisitive Mentoring Interactions	Insight Listen Give input and why Provide alternatives Take initiative	Share in responsibility for their growth
	Selected	Aware of own benefit Changes mind Selling Political probing	Cooperative Tactful Deliver on expectations	Follower is an assigned role to this leader; each has clear duties
	Earned	Respecting others Adjusting behaviors Seeks opinions Informally assess	Interaction Honest feedback Inclusion Confirm abilities	A leader is only as good as permitted by the followers

Figure 3-6

Identifying & Reacting to Leadership Philosophies

One becomes most effect as a natural leader when philosophy is compatible with leadership motive syndromes. The philosophies of Formal and Social are a basis for the application of the other four philosophies. The Formal can be applied either inside the person as in Born philosophy, or outside as in Selected philosophy. The Social philosophy can be applied inside as Maturing philosophy, or outside as in Earned philosophy. The four applied philosophies can be understood as manifestation of the four leadership syndromes as shown in Figure 3-7. When your philosophy is compatible with your leadership syndrome then the experience of leadership is natural and you can be a more effective leader. For example, when leadership is based on your own initiative as in the Born philosophy and accomplishment is of great importance, the *Innovation* syndrome provides the motivation for success. When there is a mismatch, the leadership syndrome (natural motives) will need to change (see Appendix 3), or the person will need to provide various coping mechanisms to work through the mismatch. If the person's philosophy is Born and the situation calls for an *Influencer* leader, then the person will have to learn to become more personable (affiliative) and not be too focused on achieving an outcome.

Leader	Philosophy	Motives	Leadership Syndrome
Basis	Formal	Power	
	Social	Affiliation	
Application	Born	Personal Causa Achievement	*Innovation* Leader
	Maturing	Personal Causa Affiliation	*Ambassador* Leader
	Selected	Power Achievement	*Mover* Leader
	Earned	Power Affiliation	*Influencer* Leader

Figure 3-7
Leadership Syndromes and Leadership
Philosophy

Dimension 3 - Leadership Roles

The elements of the job to be done

Leadership roles are a function of the demands of situations or circumstances. Expectations in an organization are more targeted to what needs to get done given the circumstances of the leader. Some circumstances demand attention from an overall grand perspective, some for coordination and inspiration for people, and still others for managing resources and tasks.

First, the Strategic/Executive grand leadership role concerns leadership through establishing bottom line numbers, communicating goals, and setting overall direction. Secondly, the People/Human role deals with personal people-oriented engagement to inspire or encourage them to follow a path to reach the desired outcome. Finally, the Management/Operations role involves balancing and coordinating resources and tasks required to reach a goal or goals. Here it is clear that these three roles consist of behaviors quite different from one another and require the leader to interpret the overall significance and impact of their leadership in the situation.

The Strategic/Executive grand leadership roles focus attention on large-scale planning, often in changing environments requiring interpretation of factors that could influence future performance. Also, the People/Human leadership role directs attention to people and how they interact or might interact. A person's interpretation of values and personal preferences are very important in this role. And then the Management/Operations leadership role is concerned with establishing effective processes and accomplishing tasks within constraints. These three roles are depicted within a leadership triangle in Figure 3-8. Every organizational circumstance is a combination of these three forms or roles with one usually predominant over the others.

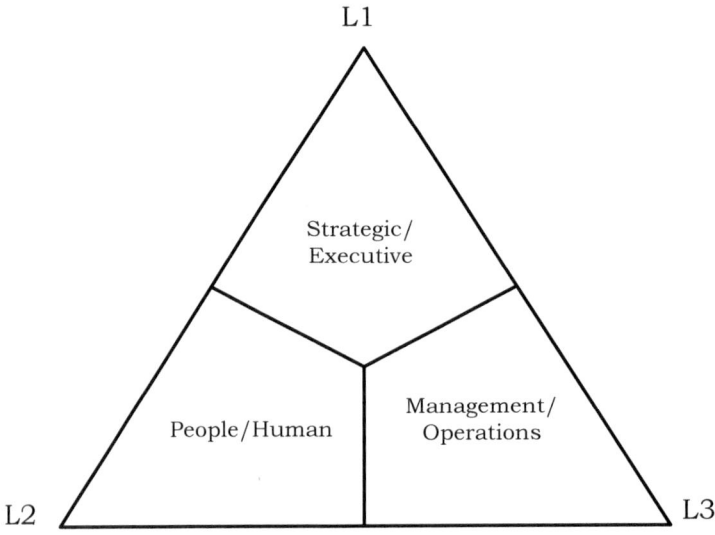

Figure 3-8
Leadership Role Triangle

    To illustrate these leadership roles, compare the uncomplicated job of moving a family from one town to another with the complex project of a space mission. Let us assume that each role of leadership will be needed for a move of a family of four with two adults and two children (one teenager and one in grade school). Strategic/Executive (L1) leadership ensures the new location can support the family financially as one of the parents secures a new job. In addition, one must consider a change to cost-of-living, schooling opportunities for the children, distance from relatives, and a variety of other important considerations. In the role of People/Human (L2) leadership there will be a focus on the well-being and adjustment of all of the family members. This could mean distance from friends, entertainment venues availability, and the comfort/pleasure or discomfort/harshness of weather conditions. Plus, a move requires the Management/Operations (L3) role of leadership due to scheduling, packing boxes, notifying utility companies and handling a variety of other incidentals. It is important that the Strategic/Executive issues be given proper attention. Nevertheless, if the family does not comply, then the move's success is unlikely. The attention given to Management/Operations (L3) leadership is minor in this situation since most moves are fairly straight forward and their processes are uncomplicated. A leader of the family move should be understanding of people and relationships with adequate skill in overall planning. This leader may even outsource the move incidentals to someone else. In this case, the leadership role is People/Human (L2).

When it comes to a mission into space, Strategic/Executive (L1) leadership is of vital importance to acquire funding and coordinate with plans on many levels. People/Human (L2) leadership is not as critical today since training and testing of astronauts has occurred for years. But Management/Operations (L3) is most critical because the operation is highly technical and requires the most diligent attention to detail. In spreading a 10-point score for importance of the leadership roles across the roles, we would have L1=3, L2=2, L3=5. The space project leader would be highly technical, an engineer at heart, along with some skill at selling the ideas to funding organizations. The People/Human (L2) leader is concerned with certain biological requirements that are needed to serve the mission.

The characteristics of the three roles of leadership are shown in Figure 3-8. Here we see that Strategic/Executive (L1) role is concerned with having a vision, selling to other people, and communicating effectively with special vocabulary. The leadership role of People/Human (L2) is focused on knowing people and their traits, self-knowledge about oneself, ability to state ideas and opinions clearly with the other person in mind, and adapting to how others like to listen. Management/Operations (L3) leadership is concerned with processes, specifically, logical relationships between tasks and how tasks are to be fulfilled. As a special case, there is a fourth leadership role identified as Indeterminant (L4). This fourth role is useful when the situation is unclear, or complex. It is difficult to select which leadership role would be best served. This leadership role, with its unexpected demands, needs to adopt skills across all three of the other roles. It requires an inquisitive nature, a relentless ability to change quickly, and skill in exhibiting agility as the situation unfolds. In some cases, the leader may have to change from one role to the next without ever establishing a predominant role. (See Figure 3-9.)

Strategic/Executive (L1)	People/Human (L2)

1. Vision
  - Know the vision of the enterprise
  - Attach current objective to the vision
  - Communicate the vision
2. Selling
  - Be able to convince others of vision's value
  - Know competing visions
  - Gain approvals from others
3. Communications
  - Communicate in ways others are able to hear and understand
  - Communicate through the appropriate vocabulary
  - Utilize normal communication patterns
  - Create new communication patterns and channels
	1. Traits
	  - Know traits of people
	  - Diagnose attitudes
	  - Assess interests of oneself and others
	  - Know how others prefer to work
	2. Self-Knowledge
	  - Know impressions you exhibit
	  - Know common personality traits
	  - Know emotional states
	3. Social interactions
	  - Share personal and professional information
	  - State opinions clearly (not forcefully)
	  - Know social mores
	4. Adaptability
	  - Assess others quickly and adapt
	  - Dialogue with others appropriately
	  - Adjust behavior based on current state of affairs

Figure 3-9
Roles of Leadership

Management/Operations (L3)	Indeterminant (L4)

1. Objective
  - Seeing from a logical
    point of view
  - Identify timeframe
  - Assess flexibility
2. Tasks
  - Establish schedule of
    tasks
  - Identify level of detail for
    tasks
  - Assign people with
    appropriate skills
3. People
  - Know roles that are
    needed
  - Identify skills of people
  - Know availability
4. Unknowns
  - Identify contingencies
  - Assess risks
  - Provide a change budget
	Inquisitive
	Changing
	Agile

Figure 3-9 - continued
Roles of Leadership

Strategic/Executive Leadership Role (L1) Examples

In business enterprises senior leaders are responsible for how they will compete in their market. Many pursue this as a serious activity and set the stage for a successful outcome. Wal Mart is a great example of planning to compete in the retail market as a low-cost provider. Saks Fifth Avenue would not be expected competition for them, so they have taken over small discount retailers, such as, Kreske (later as K-Mart) through aggressive negotiations in product purchasing coupled with excellent supply-chain logistics.

Failure to plan, many have said, is planning to fail. The computer disk drive market is a good example of failure to plan. The demand for disk drives changed dramatically when smaller computers and personal computers became prevalent. Companies that were producing disk drives for major mainframe computers are no longer in business. They missed the market due to poor planning.

Through another example, every sailing ship company which crossed the oceans failed because they missed the importance of the steam engine in their poor planning.

"Count the cost" is a tenet of effective planning. If you ever remodel your home, it is best to assess what you can afford before walls are removed and materials are ordered. Most plan remodeling in phases in which each remodel phase is planned and justified on its own with an overall eye on a larger plan. As noted, many circumstances require leaders to function in the Strategic/Executive (L1) role.

People/Human Leadership Role (L2) Examples

Leaders know that working with people can be rewarding or unrewarding. Anyone can find it difficult to get along with others even if we consider them "normal" and not subject to abnormal tendencies. Often business managers provide personality tests for their employees to reveal personal preferences in the hope that if one understands the other, they may work better together (see Chapter 2). Someone who is extroverted may find it difficult to work with an introvert unless they understand that introversion is their "way" and is irrelevant to the quality of their relationship.

In another example, there was a leader who was seldom in his office and difficult to reach in spite of being on the premises daily. He preferred this approach so that new spontaneous interactions were held to a minimum. He gave the impression of someone aloof and judgmental, but actually he was simply more guarded in his interactions than most people. Once identified as someone who tended to be introverted, interactions with him improved greatly.

Understanding others is critical in many situations, such as, dating, marriage and parenting. One needs to understand the other person as a person, not as a role played out against a defined set of rules or guidelines. People often use formalities to side-step the need to understand a person as a person. Job descriptions are often used to mistakenly describe the person who would be effective or successful in a job, rather than customizing the role to suit the individual. As an example, it is notable and clear when tracking an order that the person helping you would be better assigned a job requiring little human interaction. No matter the issue, you have the impression that it is all your problem; and the sooner you are off the phone, the better it would be for them. On the other hand, when you do encounter someone helpful, a people person, it can brighten your day. This employee's personality was likely considered before assigning them a job. To be successful in many situations, leaders need to know people as people, not as roles to be performed.

Management/Operations Leadership Role (L3) Examples

When the performance of processes is important, the role of Manager/Operations supervisor should be stressed. Processes can make a difference in how well a business delivers its services or products. For example, some businesses compete on quality rather than on cost or small market segments. In order to produce quality, there needs to be a concern for the processes in place to monitor and improve quality. Process leadership in quality has become very popular.

The Malcolm Baldrige National Quality Award is an example of the importance of process leadership. The award was established by the U.S. Congress in 1987 to raise awareness of quality process management and recognize American companies that have implemented successful quality management systems. According to the foundation "The award is the nation's highest presidential honor for performance excellence." When processes are executed in excellent ways, great things can happen.

It was a memorable day when Captain "Sully" Sullenberger skillfully landed US Airways Flight 1549 onto the Hudson River. He saved the lives of 155 passengers and crew. It was not just luck. He had been training all his professional life to be an excellent aircraft pilot from his junior piloting experiences to his professional training in the United States Air Force. His training included commercial passenger aircraft and reviews of air disasters or near disasters. Soon after takeoff his aircraft hit a flock of birds and all engines stopped and could not be restarted. He had almost no time to make a decision to avoid a disaster and choose the best alternative for the plane and its passengers. Landing on the Hudson River was his solution and proved to be the best. His process training and process leadership in this situation resulted in this positive outcome. Later in simulations it was shown that if he had turned back, he would have crashed in populated areas with no aircraft survivors. Some situations call for process leadership and can even result in life-or-death outcomes, as with Sully and his decision to land on the Hudson River.

In another example, master gardeners with outstanding flower gardens are often very process oriented. They must manage their gardens with proper and timely feeding, watering, and protections against weather and insects. The beauty of their gardens is enjoyable due to their care and management of processes.

Indeterminant Leadership Role (L4) Examples

This leadership role can be described as entrepreneurial or innovative. Here one must determine if solid planning, concern for human interaction, or an attention to managing processes is needed. Often any decision, even if wrong, seems the only escape from a complex, unforeseen dilemma. Feedback from initial leadership actions is critical and evaluation of them must be done to determine what happened as a result of them.

As an example, in announcing candidacy for a political office, the reaction of the constituency will dictate whether to plan an intricate campaign, reach out to individuals for support, or establish a campaign headquarters to handle all the materials. It may be unclear at first what may be needed, thus "indeterminant." It is possible all will be needed.

The COVID-19 experience in 2020-2021 is another example of unclear leadership. Leadership in companies was ill defined at the beginning of the crisis and kept changing as events unfolded. While many companies folded due to circumstances beyond their control, others folded because they we unable to lead with agility. Those companies with agile, creative leaders made it through the crisis and thrived. Many companies were able to pivot to a new reality, but others were unable to take the risky steps that would allow them to survive.

When a leadership opportunity is filled with a person whose natural leadership syndrome is compatible with the opportunity, there is better chance for a successful outcome. The importance of communication and the sense of overall control in the Strategic/Executive role makes the *Influencer* leader most appropriate for these circumstances. On the other hand, the People/Human circumstance needs communication but also energy to initiate individual interactions as in an *Ambassador* leader. The Management/Operations circumstances requires overall control along with a good sense of accomplishment as is in the *Mover* leader. The Indeterminant role of leadership requires an overall sense of accomplishment coupled with taking initiative which makes it most appropriate for the *Innovation* leader. (See Figure 3-10.)

Leadership Roles	Motives	Leadership Syndrome
Strategic Executive	Power Affiliation	*Influencer* Leader
People Human	Personal Causation Affiliation	*Ambassador* Leader
Management Operations	Power Achievement	*Mover* Leader
Indeterminant	Personal Causation Achievement	*Innovation* Leader

Figure 3-10
Leadership Roles and Leadership Syndromes

Summary

Leadership has a variety of meanings. In an organization the organizational culture can provide an insight into what motives would be most natural for a leader. Also, for each individual, leadership has a personal meaning, as in a philosophy, a deeply held belief. Leadership can also be a looked on as a role bounded by the leader's circumstances. These circumstances can be strategic, people, management, or indeterminant. Motives can be combined into leadership syndromes. Each provides energy along with a focus for that energy. When the leadership motive syndromes of *Mover, Influencer, Innovator,* or *Ambassador* are compatible with organizational culture, personal philosophy, and the leader's circumstances; you, as the leader, can act in natural ways producing a feeling of comfort and harmony. Leadership syndromes, as revealed by motives, reveal compatibility opportunities across the various leadership notions giving you the opportunity to be a natural leader. An *Influencer* syndrome would be compatible in an Organized culture, a Maturing philosophy, and Strategic circumstance. The *Mover* syndrome would be compatible with a Target culture, a Selected philosophy, and a Management circumstance. The *Innovation* syndrome would be compatible with an Entrepreneurial culture, a Born philosophy, and an Indeterminant circumstance. The *Ambassador* syndrome would be compatible with a Familial culture, an Earned philosophy, and a People circumstance (See Figure 3-11.)

This has been an examination of leadership syndromes across the notions of culture, leadership philosophy, and leadership roles.

Leadership Dimensions				Influencer (Power, Affiliation)	Mover (Power, Achievement)	Innovator (Pers Causation, Achievement)	Ambassador (Pers Causation, Affiliation)
Roles	The Job		Indeterminant			X	
			Operations		X		
			People				X
			Strategic	X			
Philosophy	Self-View		Earned				X
			Selected		X		
			Maturing	X			
			Born			X	
Culture	The Company		Familial				X
			Entrepreneurial			X	
			Ordered	X			
			Target		X		

Figure 3-11
Leadership Syndromes and Leadership
Dimensions

It would be very fortunate to have all these motivational elements line up perfectly. However, when this is not the case, then the effective leader must become active by learning the appropriate motives, or lead in nonconforming or unnatural ways as possible. If your dominant motives are *power* and *affiliation* you have the *Influencer* syndrome. If your personal philosophy is *Maturing* and your leadership role is *Strategic* your motives are compatible with your environment. However, if the culture of the organization is *Target* then you would have a problem using your natural *affiliation* motive when it comes to dealing with people across the organizational culture. The organization would be more concerned with meeting goals than developing relationships in order to meet business objectives. In other words, you would have to change your approach to one of meeting goals rather than building relationships.

So, as discussed, we can see leadership can be understood as a social reality through understanding organizational culture, a fact of personal philosophy, as well as roles that are driven by circumstances. The common foundation for leadership is that which interests a person as shown by motive syndromes. Strong, natural leadership comes down to the internal preference for action – one's motives, coupled with learning how to accommodate mismatches culturally, personally, and circumstantially.

Motives in Your Life

Chapter 4

Motives and Careers

What cruel mistakes are sometimes made by benevolent men and women in matters of business about which they know nothing and think they know a great deal.

Florence Nightingale

Introduction

In the work world many remain with one company happily and often in the same job for an entire career. Others move from company to company and job to job never finding job satisfaction. So, when people are initiating or realigning their careers, not only do they examine the current job tasks but they study how they are a natural fit for a work environment. It is two-fold; they look for environments that will let them use their skills and abilities, as well as let them naturally express their attitudes and values. Motives are the basis of attitudes and values and knowing them provides an insight on which career might be most self-rewarding. When people are engaged in self-rewarding careers, they tend to stay in them longer and meet with more success. Motives are the basis of fulfilling careers. Of course, being able to adequately perform the tasks is critical. Beyond that, having the energy to engage with these tasks in a way that is natural, tends to make work-life more fulfilling and something one can look forward to rather than feeling uneasy, stressed, and unrewarded.

Professional Scenarios

Often people begin an initial career only to discover later that it does not suit their natural tendencies and acquired skills. They have grown beyond their initial job choice. They become so preoccupied with the day-to-day job itself that they rarely reflect on their current circumstance. The following is an example.

Gene is now a dynamic senior project manager at Largo Tools and is driving to work and reflecting on his ten-year career at Largo. The trip usually takes about 20 minutes, that is, when he speeds just a little. He loves his job and anticipates that today should be rewarding since he is meeting with the major stakeholders on his new product launch project. While driving he reconsiders the unsatisfying years lost doing an engineering job he eventually discovered was no longer a good fit for him. After parking his car, he bounds up the stairs to his office while greeting people on the way.

Recalling his engineering studies and his 10-year career as an engineer at Largo, Gene began to wonder why he got into engineering in the first place. He considered "I spent a great deal of my professional life with my head in the computer working out really cool design solutions. The challenge of finding the most appropriate solution gets me excited, and the bonuses are not bad either. However, it seems like I was always somewhat isolated from the rest of the people at Largo. Why was that? Largo is a great company, voted one of the top five employers in the metro area. They are first rate in every way - friendly, kind, and helpful. And management is really good at getting people lined up with their strengths. It is like a close-knit family and I really like this place, but something wasn't right for me and I wasn't feeling good about my job"

Gene's thoughts drifted to his dad who was excellent at designing boxes and package solutions for his customers. He and his partner were very successful in their small business. It must have been terrific for him. I remember our talks that resulted in him sending me off to engineering school hoping lots of doors would be open for me professionally. Glad I listened to his advice. Engineering school was perfect for me; I learned how to use my good math skills to solve real-life problems." Gene was recruited his senior year with job offers from three very good companies. He chose Largo, not only for the money, but for the way the recruiters represented this genuine and down to earth company. He felt like he could ask them anything and get a straight answer. Yet even in his senior year with great job offers, he briefly thought of ignoring all his engineering education and taking a low-level stage manager job for a local repertory theatre company. He helped direct a few plays on campus with the drama department and really liked the interaction and excitement. He viewed it as a technical problem that could be worked out with real live people. However, using his own reasoning along with advice from his father, he focused on an engineering career and pushed aside the idea of being a stage manager.

Eight years into his career, he had second thoughts and moved from pure engineering to project management to run the new product launch project. Until he assumed the new product launch project, he was unaware of how his engineering job had become a burden overtime. In his first couple of years with

Largo, he arrived early and stayed late about every day. His reason was not to impress anyone but to enjoy what he was doing – achieving success after success with his engineering skills. That was the past. Just before he took on running the new product launch project, he often came in a little late and caught himself watching the clock so he might beat some of the traffic on the way home. The longer he worked at his engineering job, the more dissatisfied he seemed to be. Gene was wondering why he had become so uninspired and just muddled-through those years. Previously he had passed up an opportunity to lead a small project on redesigning the customer feedback process. The project was not a pure engineering project but one that would have combined his design skills with what he felt was missing, an interaction with people from other departments and customers. So, when the new product launch project job became available, a job that combined design skills and interdepartmental coordination, he took it. The new product launch project enabled him to realize his true aspirations. He realized that passing up the redesign of the customer feedback process could have been an earlier career building opportunity. Why was he so blind as not to see I what he needed? Taking his dad's advice to study engineering made sense because it opened the door to this great company. However, being unaware of his natural personal interests in interacting with people cost him several years of unsatisfying work and late entry into a more fulfilling career.

In another example, a young woman was good at design and chose a career in fashion design. After attending a prestigious school and working over five years in fashion design, she began to consider a new career direction. As a result, she returned to school to study how to become a project manager. After her academic success, she accepted a job in a technical area for a large enterprise. She was readily promoted to a strategic project area. Soon she and her bosses discovered her real interest was in communicating and collaborating with people. This was evident initially in her career as a fashion designer, but later in working with all sorts of people involved in strategic projects. Managing technical projects is mostly about communicating really well which she did successfully. She had stepped back to take inventory of her career and had made a great choice. If she had been given the opportunity to examine her career often within a five-year span, she could have made the change sooner to begin building her new career.

The Knowing-Living Gap

Betraying one's own natural inclinations or preferences in viewing a career or potential career produces a knowing-living gap. A knowing-living gap represents one's own view of a professional career as "in-the-knowing", as compared to that which motivates one naturally as "in-the-living". When a career complements one's natural motives, one is excited about it, just as Gene in the story above was motivated when he started as an engineer. He had grown in his need for affiliation but had not assessed how his motives had evolved. Choosing a career without considering one's natural motives could be an initial mistake that could take years to recover. Even if the career choice has a valid motive basis, it may change over time. To make matters worse many people choose what they think is their preference when it may not be so naturally. What people thoughtfully claim as personal preferences are often not what they experience when living out these preferences. A thoughtful choice made at the present time about our future often turns out to not be what we really wanted. Consider our choices for automobile preferences, selections off a menu for dinner, clothing purchases, and, primarily, a choice of a career that we see as perfect. Wrong or poor career choices can cost years of discontent and stress. Simply put, it is likely that what we think we want, we really do not want. We create a fiction about ourselves and even the opportunity at hand. Fortunately, there is potential help when it comes to making career choices.

Living a preference is decidedly different from stating one. There can be serious consequences to this knowing-living gap. We can easily overcome a bad dinner choice or that odd shirt purchase (that looked so good in the store), but a bad career choice may take years to overcome. The gap's effect on ourselves and others may put us in circumstances so outside of our own real preferences so that we may never find out what we are naturally suited to do. We should try to get our natural preferences correct at the beginning of a career opportunity, and assess motives over time to see if there have been changes.

Gene started a career requiring little interaction with people only to find out later he would like to have more of it. He became more considerate of interactions with people, but not necessarily more effective with them. Gene spent several more years not fully realizing his need. Effective people skills training could have significantly reduced his learning time. Using an assessment to identify his natural motives, he could have pursued a new career track earlier. Thus, to live in a more natural way within a career, one should assess one's own natural motives with repeated assessment every few years.

Motive Syndromes and Careers

When a person is in a career that fits their skills and abilities along with their motives, people around them are usually happy to work with them or participate in their role. As an example, when you call the help-desk and you interact with someone who fits the help desk job in ability and motivation, it usually is a pleasure to receive the help. From a different angle, you go through a fast-food drive-through but receive the wrong sandwich. Inside the establishment you meet an unsympathetic manager who abruptly states "I'll fix it," and then throws it in the trash. You hope the next one is correct. No apology or respect is shown to you as the customer. This is a business run without the *affiliation* motive and it shows in the behavior of their employees. Relationships with customers in the fast-food service industry need to be honored even if only in some small ways.

A syndrome is a set of things that, taken together, define a new category. Within the four motives, there are motive-level combinations that map into career performance. Six career performance motive syndromes have been identified. Career motive syndromes are a weighted combination of the four motives of *achievement, affiliation., power,* and *personal causation.* Certain types of careers are best performed when an individual possesses a particular motive syndrome. Each of the motives are measured as low, medium, or high see figure 4-1.

Career Performance Motive Syndromes	Syndrome	Motives			
		Achievement	Affiliation	Power	Personal Causation
Coordinating	Socializer⁻	Medium	Medium	Low	Medium
Mutuality	Socializer⁺	High	High	Low	Medium
Directing	Doer⁻	Medium	Medium	High	Low
Initiating	Overcomer	High	Medium	Low	High
Controlling	Persuader	High	High	High	Medium
Leading	Agent	Medium	Medium	High	High

Figure 4-1
Career Motive Syndromes
- = Weak, + = Strong

The **Coordinating syndrome** is concerned with open and interactive communication. It involves connecting people and things as well as information. Careers with this syndrome include clerical/office worker, receptionist, editor, research assistant, scheduler, loan processor, paralegal, and registrar. For instance, a clerical/office worker often has to work with others to accomplish their tasks such as assembling documents, scheduling meetings, supporting office machines in concert with others, handling publications, and informing others about office guidelines in addition to acting as a conduit from various managers to their subordinates. Job titles for this position could be executive assistant, private secretary, staff assistant, and office manager. When in this career as a natural, this person makes everyone around them much more productive, plus they initiate tasks that others may forget or ignore. Credit for their excellent work may often go unnoticed since they simply make others look good. When someone is in a career that is not natural for them, the results are much different. They may have problems being timely, they may be disgruntled if someone asks them to do more or other work than they had planned, and they may take on tasks that are outside their purview, perhaps in a way to control others.

Career performance for coordinating careers requires a moderate level of *affiliation.* Here one is dealing with others but not responsible for establishing and maintaining relationships. Also, a moderate level of *achievement* is critical since they need to get things done but their job is usually more routine and therefore not high in a need to set new goals to achieve. Plus, a low level of *power* is set in motion since they usually are following guidelines set by others and do not feel disrespected when they are not influential in setting or changing such guidelines. Lastly, a medium in *personal causation* is needed since they may have to initiate some actions such as reminding others of tasks.

The **Mutuality syndrome** involves knowing yourself and the other person to make a good connection. Building and sustaining relationships with others is critical while accomplishing a goal personally or corporately established. Examples of careers requiring mutuality are investment counseling; account executive; minister; alumni development specialist; management of a large benevolent enterprise (e.g., United Way); field representative (as in corporate control with franchisees); and sustained sales. People good at mutuality find ways to manage themselves when encountering others. They are boundary-spanners connecting people from two differing environments. They can adjust their style or presentation of themselves to another person or people – one quality of high Self-Monitors. Self-Monitors read a situation and the people in it to present themselves and what they represent in a good light. These people have the ability to imitate the behavior of others, hide true feelings about someone, adjust quickly to the needs of a situation, and make impromptu presentations or speeches. They often are accused of being social chameleons who change their opinions based on who is present and the situation. They build many friendships but find it hard to have deep relationships. Yet they bring people together in ways for which those involved are very grateful and usually quite pleased.

Mutuality requires a strong *affiliative* motive and a strong *achievement* motive. Building, growing and sustaining relationships is critical for this sort of career, as well as achieving sales targets. *Power* is not of concern since controlling others provides little impact and may even get in the way of the mutuality required in trusted relationships. However, moderate *personal causation* is needed to be creative in building and sustaining these relationships.

As an example, Mutuality comes into play when performing sustained sales functions for a business. This sort of sales function is grounded in the relationships of customers/clients and not just in the selling of a good or service to a one-time buyer. The customers/clients' life positions and assumptions need to be considered in order to establish good mutual relationships. Also, an outcome needs to be achieved that is beneficial for the business, while at the same time ensuring relationships are built and maintained for the customers/clients. Sustaining sales is a two-sided proposition.

The **Directing syndrome** is as its name indicates – a comfortable 'take charge" of a situation. Here one focuses on directing people while achieving an overall goal.   Examples of this career syndrome include some healthcare professionals; performance directing (e.g., stage, film, orchestra); and clinical psychology. One must be able to provide opportunities for others to experience fulfilling work while ensuring that goals and expectations are met. This requires a high *power* motive. Standards and "rules of play" are important and need to be understood and communicated to others, namely, how these standards affect others as well as their responsibility to them. There is little room for innovation or creativity, therefore, low in *personal causation*. People are important and need consideration but not to the degree wherein they overwhelm what needs to be done, that is, medium in *affiliation* motive. Accomplishing specific tasks ranks high but does not obstruct the overall impact, as in medium in *achievement* motive. Further examples that require Directing are sports manager, sports team captain,

111

coach, fire commander, nurse, manager, operating medical doctor, high school principal, and orchestra director. When "very good" Directing people shows up, it usually indicates that those they direct come out on top. This could be in a sports area where they have winning records, in business as in outstanding restaurant ratings, or an orchestra that celebrated excellent performances and recordings.

Power is needed so that the expected outcome is prioritized above other considerations. However, Directing involves bringing other people on board which means having acquired the requisite formal authority along with earned authority from those being directed. This earned authority can be acquired by gaining the trust of those being directed. Trust is most effectively acquired by simply listening. Once you can understand what is "in it for them", you can direct them in ways that are beneficial for them to achieve the overall outcome. Skill in the art of listening plus the knowledge of what is needed will produce results.

One example of Directing is a nurse who has the patient's overall health in mind–while providing personal engagement to get the patient to abide by the health regimen recommended. Some patients may not want to take certain medication or even admit to an illness. The nurse needs to find a way to work through situations so that the patient ends up healthier after treatment. The nurse needs the requisite knowledge as well as trust from the patient. Listening to the patient not only provides health information but begins to establish trust.

Another example would be a basketball coach who encourages players to practice or condition themselves in certain ways to produce a positive impact for the entire team. The coach has to gain the trust of the player in a personal manner and ensure they actually meet performance expectations. A player's contribution is of overriding importance to the overall team success.

The **Initiating syndrome** involves action on one's own accord to accomplish a specific goal or goals. Examples of careers with this syndrome are information technologist (e.g., programmer, technical analyst); engineering, researcher; marketing; air traffic control; fashion designer; and advertising. Some careers require an "Initiating" person, someone to be a first mover, who is not waiting for others to start an activity. These Initiator-type careers can be fulfilling for some since the person has direct responsibility for an accomplishment through special skills or insights. Insights and skills can be in the form of technical expertise as in engineering or information technology, with an understanding of markets and competition as in marketing and advertising. When presented with a difficult problem, they will pursue a solution without being told to do so, and often work over and above expectations until the solution is achieved. Motivationally one needs to be high in *personal causation* and *achievement*, at least medium in *affiliation*, yet with only low need for *power*. Initiating encompasses sacrificial commitment and setting personal goals.

Computer Programmers are tasked with a solution to write a system that would keep track of all customer data and produce management reports. This would be an example of the initiator. They diligently produce results, often working extra hours to meet personal and other deadlines, while relying on their expertise. Once completed many people may refer to the result by name as "Frank's" or "Mary's" system. In a different light the engineers who quickly designed a unique solution to bring astronauts back from the Apollo 13 mission, a mission that almost ended in disaster, employed their natural motivation.

113

Long hours, quick decisioning and innovation, and a drive with a high sense of achievement were imperative for success.

The **Controlling syndrome** uses influence and personal energy to achieve goals. Examples of careers with this syndrome are: project manager; business department manager; specializing medical doctor; airline pilot captain; and managing editor. Controlling careers require that the person primarily takes charge of others within the environment and pursues with equal importance the goal or goals required. A high *power* motive along with a high *achievement* motive are needed. High *affiliation* motive is needed since relationships with people are useful for achieving outcomes, along with a medium need for *personal causation* since creativity or innovation may be necessary in some of these careers.

Often a team structure is needed to accomplish the goals. Teams must establish a personal identity, agree to a set of team guidelines to follow, and find a way to coordinate the specialties within the team itself. The way in which the team works together is brought about by effective usage of *power*. Often adjudication of issues between team members will have to be addressed since relationship management is highly important.

For instance, with the *achievement* motive project managers need to ensure that the impact of a project is beneficial for all key stakeholders. With the *affiliation* motive an entire team produces the required deliverable. The *power* motive controls the effective usage of resources in making trade-offs between time, money, and people. As in the case of an airline pilot captain who within the *power* motive must maintain control of the entire flight, with the *affiliation* motive to keep crew and passengers settled with their respective positions, with the *achievement* motive ensure the flight reaches its destination without mishap, and with moderate *personal causation* motive steps are taken to make minor adjustments.

The **Leading syndrome** focuses on what might be considered senior leaders. Examples of careers with the Leading syndrome are Chief Executive Officer in business enterprise; school dean; head baseball manager; and other enterprise leaders (e.g., hospital, church, state governor). Here *power* and *personal causation* motives are very important. We see that with *power* these leaders need to act while keeping others in mind, with *personal causation* they need to initiate their leadership behavior and not merely react to present circumstances, with *affiliation* they need to bring others on board with their ideas, and with *achievement* they need to have a managerial structure that attends to meeting required objectives for the mission established. These leaders are required to be emotionally self-aware, be able to manage their own emotions, be socially aware of situations and people, and be able to establish relationships with a variety of people. One discovers results in personal transparency, partnerships with other enterprises, quick remodeling of current enterprises, and the initiation of new ways of thinking for those who are a part of these enterprises.

The CEO of a business enterprise is an example of a career with the Executive Management (Leading) syndrome. Leaders are responsible for establishing the mission of their enterprise. They understand their business, its products and services, and how they will compete with others. They must determine whether or not they compete as a low-cost provider, as a high-quality provider, or as an enterprise with a niche in a market. A managerial structure should be put into place, one with high control, with low control, or with a distribution of duties by product or geographically. They establish how they can ensure the enterprise will be sustained over a long period of time. This could be through product innovation, talent management, and/or outside consultation.

The senior leader in a hospital is another example of Executive Management (Leading) career syndrome. One establishes a mission around how to provide healthcare for all people or a certain selected group. They may "compete" by exclusive services; special services (e.g., cancer treatment); or by locations(s). Leaders establish a management structure that is keyed to volume and high control, or one that is more driven by compassionate services to its specialized patients.

The relationship between these careers and motive syndromes is shown below.

Career Motive Syndromes	Careers	Achievement	Affiliation	Power	Personal Causation
				Motives	
Coordinating	Clerical/Office Worker Receptionist Editor Researcher Assistant Scheduler Loan Processor Paralegal Registrar	Medium	Medium	Low	Medium
Mutuality	Investment Counseling Account Executive Minister Alumni Development Specialist Management of a large benevolent enterprise Field Representative Sustained Sales	High	High	Low	Medium
Directing	Nursing Coaching Performance directing (stage, film) Clinical Psychology	Medium	Medium	High	Low

Figure 4-2

Career Motive Syndromes and Motives

Career Motive Syndromes	Careers	Motives			
		Achievement	Affiliation	Power	Personal Causation
Initiating	Information Technologist Engineering Researcher Marketing Air Traffic Control Advertising	High	Medium	Low	High
Controlling	Project Manager Business Department Manager Specializing medical doctor Airline Pilot Captain Managing Editor	High	High	High	Medium
Leading	Chief Executive Officer School Dean Head Baseball Manager Other enterprise leader (E.G., hospital, churches, state governors)	Medium	Medium	High	High

Figure 4-2
Career Motive Syndromes and Motives - continued

When Gene, in the previous example, decided to change from engineer to project manager, he moved from an *Initiating* syndrome to a *Controlling* syndrome. He went from a medium career need for *affiliation* to a high need for *affiliation*, and from a low need for *power* to a high need for *power*. He may have had these higher needs in *affiliation* and *power* all along, as witnessed by his involvement earlier as a stage manager in a repertory theatre. However, his motives of *achievement* and *personal causation* were of a priority being reinforced by his engineering career choice and his father's encouragement. Some natural motives are often masked by other natural motives or opinions of those around us. Gene's career path to project manager could have been begun earlier if he was more aware of his natural motives.

By knowing your career motive syndrome, it is possible to see if the career you are in, or hope to be in, is compatible with your natural motives. When the opportunities in your career or job are compatible with your natural motives then that career can lead to a feeling of self-fulfillment providing a possible path to success. Also, some frustrations in a career or on a job can be explained when there is an incompatibility between your career and your natural motives. Knowing your natural motives and your desired career, you have the opportunity to change one or the other, or both. Suppose you wanted to be a project manager but through a motives analysis you found out that you lacked the level of *achievement* needed. It is possible to be trained in *achievement* to meet the requirement. However, if you were assessed high in *power* and *affiliation* natural motives you might aspire to a *Leading* career, perhaps as a senior manager in an operational area of your business. Building an effective career can begin with knowing your natural motives. With this knowledge you can make wise choices between career opportunities, as well as know what motive training, if any, might be most beneficial for you.

Chapter 5

Motives and Choices

Good judgment comes from experience, and a lot of that comes from bad judgment.

Will Rogers

In this chapter we will look at situations we all face in life that call for making a decision or choosing between alternatives. The Behavior Potential in these situations differs by the kind of motives that you have. Motives that are oriented more toward rational processes help explain one kind of choice activity, and those that are more oriented toward relationships explain another. Behavioral Economics highlights why some people use rational processes and some do not when choosing between alternatives. Once motives are understood resolving disputes among people who differ in their method for choosing can be much more efficient. The following is a story that will be used to show how people apply different methods for choosing between alternatives.

Buying a House Story

George and Marie along with Uncle Leonard were gathering at 6:30 p.m., as was their tradition, for their daily evening meal. After their initial discussion of how their day had been spent, they began to talk about their house and the possibility of buying one for the three of them. Each of them had a different point of view about another house. George indicated he really did not care about location as long as it made financial sense, in that it did not cost too much, and that it was in an area close to their work. In the back of his mind, he also would like to have a place where he could fulfill his desire for horseback riding. Marie really wanted to find a very nice neighborhood that was open to new people, and was easy for people to get to know one another. She was suggesting perhaps a self-contained, organized neighborhood community. Uncle Leonard voiced no preferences but he just knew that there was a certain amount of time, effort, and finances that had to go into making a move. So, while he somewhat agreed with George, he also was very open-minded and more creative in thinking and finding another house. Arguments went on about who wanted what, when, and where for most of the meal. Since they were not getting any closer to a consensus, they decided to table the discussion and contact a realtor.

Uncle Leonard had been thinking earlier "my niece was so kind to take me in after my stroke, but now that all is well, I am not sure what my future holds with the family in a move. I would really like to continue as a close part of the family but need to find a way to make a meaningful contribution". Marie and George really like him and it would please them a great deal if he continued to live with them.

After graduating with an advanced degree, George began working for a pharmaceutical company researching new forms of relieving pain associated with muscle soreness and debilitation. Before he began working for the pharmaceutical company, he and a friend developed a new physical therapeutic process for lower back pain. They received a patent on the process and it became very popular. Consequently, George finds himself in a well-paid job with significant income from both his job and his patented process, so his house budget was fairly high.

When George was 25, he married Marie who was going through medical school. She now practices as an OB/GYN, and is on staff at one of the city's leading hospitals. She and George raised two children who have now moved on to another community and are well established in their professional and personal lives. They come home to visit on holidays and special occasions and get along with their parents quite well. Marie's substantial income also means the budget for another house can be on the high side.

Uncle Leonard, has been living with them since his stroke but is now fully recovered. He seems to fill a void for George and Marie after their kids left, and they so much enjoy his stories and accounts of the various people he used to deal with for over 30 years as a stage show director. He enjoys a hefty retirement income and insists on making a large financial contribution to the family budget. He also is a great help with household chores including walking and feeding their pet beagle, Loafer.

George, Marie, and Uncle Leonard now find themselves riding around with Whitney, their realtor, looking at houses. George wants a reasonably-priced large house with a stable so he can realize his dream of owning a horse. Marie wants a large house in a managed neighborhood community, while Uncle Leonard would like a large mansion that could be remodeled to suit their needs. Whitney's opinion is they can find what they want in a nice well-established neighborhood since they would get much more "bang for their buck."

Not only do they not agree on the best kind of house, they are approaching the choice in different ways. George sees the choice as a rational process involving location, size, upkeep, and price. Marie has a much more open process since she knows they can afford almost anything within reason. She considers the importance of their neighbors, how their kids would feel about their purchase since they come to visit often, and how she could host get-togethers with family and friends. She also wishes to be close to restaurants and other social venues so they could make new friends. Uncle Leonard wants them to have discussions to brainstorm what they each would like to have, then set up a series of family meetings to negotiate them, and then compromise to form a "must-have" list along with a list of what each member would like to have in their new house. Whitney's process for choosing a house is to show them a large number of different houses and have them each identify the two or three they could live with, and then choose the best overall.

Last week Marie and Whitney were looking at a home that Marie thought was perfect because of its location but it was offered at a price well over similar houses in similar places throughout the city. Whitney explained that people put more value on their houses than they are worth for a couple of reasons. One, to start the negotiation at a higher price thinking people will "go from there", and two, many really believe the increase in value over market value is appropriate since they have precious memories which unwittingly place a financial value on them. They were about to make what they thought was a reasonable offer on this overpriced home but Marie wanted to keep looking for a more perfect house. George then came up with another house that he thought was far more fitting to their needs. It was located close to their jobs and had more rooms, a pool, a circle drive and was a little less than their agreed-on budget. After Marie left work, she and Whitney went to see it and Marie vetoed the suggestion. She thought the street did not have a good feel since the neighbors seemed to be to spread out making it hard to get to know them. She remembers where she grew up and how it was a warm and comforting neighborhood where people knew each other, and looked out for one another. She still sees her friends socially from the old neighborhood. George does not have many of these kinds of friends which tends to make Marie delay in choosing a new house. Marie also feels she is putting more effort into the search than George or Uncle Leonard.

When Marie got home, she could not find Uncle Leonard and began to worry. Just as she was about to call George, who was working late, Uncle Leonard showed up with Loafer who had run off. He said the dog reminded him of one of his starlets who kept going out the backstage door with one of the trumpet players. He recalled how he had to manage not only production details but the people as well. Per Uncle Leonard's request Marie agreed to meet with him with George that night to come up with a list for what they really wanted in a house.

The next day Uncle Leonard called Whitney and they began to whittle down the possibilities. They found three houses that seemed to fit the bill. After a brief tour of the three houses, Uncle Leonard became very upset about the prices and the amount of work needed. There was one house he thought was really perfect. While the house was well within their budget, it needed much updating which would put it over their budget limit. After Whitney pointed out the value of a construction loan, and the much lower taxes as a result of a grant for stimulating property updates, it became the lead contender. The house satisfied many of the "must-haves." Marie got what she wanted since there were nice neighbors that had invested significant amounts of money in their houses, along with the opportunity to make new friends by participating in a neighborhood beautification program. George ran the numbers and was pleased with the financials and the short commute to work for both he and Marie, plus the fact that there was a stable less than three miles away so he could finally begin owning and enjoying a horse. In taking these points into consideration with Uncle Leonard's management skills and willingness to volunteer to "run the project," they all agreed to take on the burden of a remodel solution, and to purchase the house.

In coming back from the house, George, Marie, and Uncle Leonard were all talking excitedly at once while Whitney was driving. Even Loafer in the back seat was feeling the excitement and added his voice to the mix. As she pulled out onto the interstate highway, they all pondered over the next steps to take. Whitney said they would discuss them once back in the office. So, they continued to talk while Whitney kept her attention on driving as safe as possible. Once back in the office and after some discussion they took Whitney's advice and made a legitimate offer that was accepted. With Uncle Leonard's remodel budget plus the price of the house, their new home will be just a little over budget.

Why George, Marie, Uncle Leonard, and Whitney approached the house purchase in different ways can be explained using Behavioral Economics further revealing that the basis for their choice actions are their natural motives.

Motives and Choices

Choices can be examined from various points of view. The reasons we choose one alternative over another is important especially when considering social-based norms and expectations. There are a variety of reasons we choose one alternative over another. We choose one because it is more ethical (the right thing to do); esthetical (it looks better to us than another); pleasurable (gives us a sense of enjoyment); and prudent (given all the facts we can consider it the best and makes the most sense). The prudent choices between financial alternatives have been the basis for understanding economic behavior, and elaborate models have been created to explain these choices. Behavioral Economics is an approach to understanding choices people make, and while primarily concerned with choosing between financial alternatives, other kinds of choices based on human behavior have been explained as well. Behavioral Economics applies psychology-based explanations for these choices. Most choices actually result in outcomes that often call for second-guessing. As an example: "Did I buy the right TV, car, or make the best choice for a vacation?" Classic economic theory assumes people make choices that are completely rational and are made to produce the optimal outcome for the person making the choice. This optimal rational approach is called *expected utility*. Two men, Daniel Kahneman and Amos Tversky were the first who seriously considered economic-base choices that violated *expected utility*. They found that people often and with great consistency violate *expected utility* and took mental short-cuts, described as heuristics or biases, when it comes to making choices. These heuristics or biases seem like "gut reactions" to choosing, but they have a level of predictability yet consist of mental processes that are less than fully analytically rational. Behavioral Economics examines

127

these various kinds of short-cuts used to evaluate choices. Motives of *achievement, affiliation, power,* and *personal causation* provide explanations and insights on why choices are made rationally as well as non-rationally using short-cuts.

Kinds of Heuristics and Biases

Eight heuristics and biases are very prevalent in making choices. These are identified below along with a brief statement about each. They are explained in further detail in the sections that follow.

1. Anchor Point Bias
   (An initial number sticks in your head and you adjust from that number)
2. Representativeness Heuristic
   (Assuming an overall process needs to be random since events within it are random)
3. Availability Heuristic
   (It is easier to remember the name of a close friend than an acquaintance since it is more available in our minds)
4. Framing Bias - Gains/Losses Bias
   (Losing an amount of money has a greater negative impact over a positive impact of winning an equal amount)
5. Framing Bias – Psychological Accounting
   (Purchases are not evaluated strictly on financial criteria)
6. Multi-Tasking Bias
   (The impossibility of thinking deeply on two issues at the same time)
7. Thinking Speed Bias
   (concentrated problem-solving verses

merely quickly communicating information)
8. Endowment Bias
(What we have has a higher value to us than it has to someone else)

Heuristics and biases are rooted in the influence of a person's social world. When people are inclined more toward social realities, they usually do not rely on their rational decision-making ability and usually "go with the flow." Motives of *affiliation* (concern for relationships) and *power* (concern for influencing people) are socially based. With motives of *affiliation* and *power,* there is a direct or positive relationship between these motives and the impact of a heuristic or bias. People high in *achievement* and/or *personal causation* will have an inverse relationship between the heuristic or bias impact. In the case of *achievement,* achieving solutions to problems overcomes social consideration, thus lessening the impact of the heuristic or bias on the individual. In the case of *personal causation* maintaining a reality focus along with a strong sense of personal responsibility lessens social impact. People high in *affiliation* and/or *power* will find themselves more influenced by heuristics and biases. They are concerned with how people feel or value the choices over and above the facts that deal strictly with the evaluations themselves.

Anchor Point Bias (1)

Given all other things being equal, I would prefer to buy a TV for $400 at another store across town rather than pay $450 where I am shopping now. Yet if I am considering a car for $35,050 and the same car from a dealer across town is 35,000, I would not normally go across town to make the purchase. The reason for choosing a $50 saving on the TV and not on the car purchase is psychological and not strictly financially rational. Personal value is not just represented by an item's price. Personal value is relative to an anchor point. For the TV the anchor is $400, and for the car the anchor point is $35,000. This behavior is explained by changes in values as one gets higher in cost (See Figure 5-1).

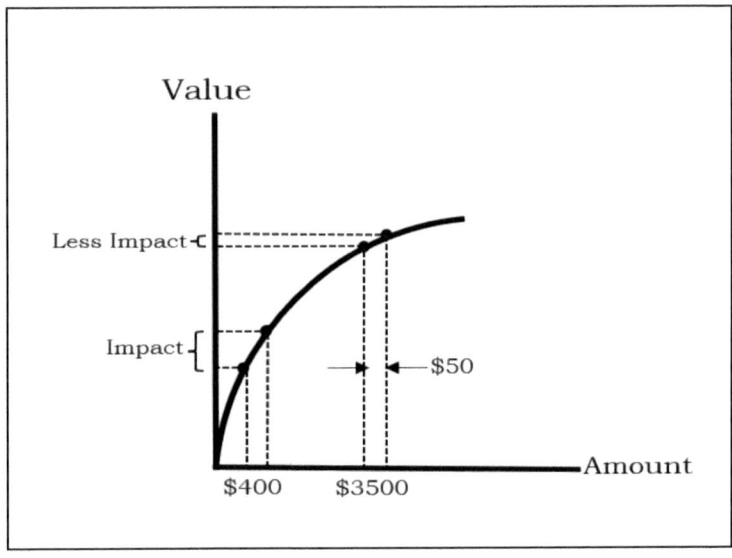

Values of Gains Verses Losses (Heuristics)
Figure 5-1

However, not all people are subject to this anchor-point bias. Some would always look for the savings regardless of the anchor point. This consistent behavior can be explained by the *achievement* motive or the *personal causation* motive. People with one or both of these motives tend to see choices in life as problems to be solved and consider them rationally, decreasing the impact of learned social influences. Those higher in *affiliation* and/or *power* motives are more likely to be influenced by relationship considerations, and their actions are more predictable taking into account the impact of heuristics and biases. (Of course, if you factor in the price of gasoline to make the drive across town, and it is equal to or greater than $50 then not making the drive would be a rational process.)

George and Whitney, in the house story, would apply the same criteria for choosing a house whether it was $70,000 or $700,000. While Marie and at times Uncle Leonard would be more influenced by the anchor point indicated, they would tend to assess the impact of going from $700,000 to $710,000 less than going from $70,000 to $80,000. These differences are explained by their motives. George and Whitney are high in *achievement* which makes them goal oriented and they interpret choices as rational problems to be solved. This blends with George's background as a researcher and Whitney's as a pragmatic realtor. Marie and uncle Leonard are high in *power* which makes them less rationally focused and susceptible to non-rational evaluation processes. Marie sees the world more as a collection of relationships, high in *affiliation* and *power*, and Uncle Leonard is good at influencing people, high in *power*, as seen by his background as a stage show director. Observing people's behavior as well as their career choices can often be a good indicator of their motives.

Representativeness Heuristic (2)

People often make choices based on what looks like a rule for randomness, but a choice that brings a process back into randomness is itself not random. An example of the *representativeness* heuristic is what people assumed to be the next result when a coin is flipped as Heads (H) or Tails (T) where previous flips came up HTHTHHH. Many people would predict the next flip being T because it looks like the result would be in keeping with a process that is random. However, the randomness of the whole process is often attributed to be *representative* of each event in it; yet the whole process itself does not abide by randomness thinking, since the next flip still remains a 50-50 chance for H or T.

Some people choose the same lottery number time after time not realizing that every other lottery number has an equal probability of being chosen as their same number, yet they choose the same number every time thinking they have increased their odds of winning. People with a high *achievement* motive have a low influence for the *representativeness* heuristic. For high *achievement* choosing is one more instance of solving a problem that they by nature approach rationally. The same is true for those high in *personal causation* since they maintain a reality focus and are not influenced by social considerations. However, those with a high *affiliation* motive would tend to look for broader human components often identifying a choice with human attributes, and therefore the heuristic would have a high influence on their behavior. Someone high in the *power* motive would also have a high influence from the *representativeness* heuristic since they tend to look at the big picture and may miss the detail limitations of the actual choice. Marie in the house purchase story would tend to think the odds of finding a perfect home would improve with added searches even if the searches were relatively the same.

Availability Heuristic (3)

The *availability* heuristic has to do with how easy something is brought to mind often ignoring the reality of the situation. An example of the *availability* heuristic is the false claim, as shown by research, that weather and arthritis are somehow connected. People remember when their arthritis "acts up" during a weather change, but discount or forget all the other times it "acted up" under normal weather conditions. Memory of these instances of weather change and arthritic pain are much more available to memory than all the other times, and can be labelled an *availability* heuristic.

When working in a group each group member usually recalls more of their percent contribution to the group than is actually the case, results of all the individual contributions add up to well over 100%. The *availability* heuristic provides a good explanation about why there may be group discord since members tend to over-attribute their contributions to positive group outcomes simply because they recall their efforts much easier than the efforts of others. High *achievement* people tend to look at the total problem and not just quickly remembered instances, so they have a low influence from the *availability* heuristic. Those high in the *personal causation* motive tend to also have a low impact from the *availability* heuristic since they have a tendency to look at the reality of the situation. Those high in *affiliation* tend to see a high impact from the *availability* heuristic since they are more concerned with relationships than efforts and contributions to outcomes. Marie in the story sees her contribution to the effort as more than was actually the case.

Framing Bias - Gains/Losses Bias

Amounts of gains versus an equal amount of loss are not judged rationally. The impact of a loss is felt greater than an equal amount of a gain. We feel worse about losing $20 than we feel good about winning $20. Outcomes that are negative, a loss, have a larger value impact for most humans than outcomes that are positive.

In one example individuals are asked to participate in a coin flip gamble. Before the game is played it is explained. The proposition is that if heads is a result of the flip the other person owes $20 to the person flipping, but if tails comes up, what value would the person have to win in order for them to actually play. Most people choose around $50. Thus, the negative value of the loss is greater than the positive value of the win. The idea of losing $20 is offset with the greater win value of $50 (see Figure 5-2).

When decisions are presented, or framed, in certain ways some people will rely on heuristics for choosing. When faced with breakfast cereal to be purchased with the box reading 90% fat free, a person is more likely to choose it over one that says 10% fat, although they both convey the same information. The 90% fat free is a gain for someone dieting, and the 10% fat is a loss. When a company has investment money, it matters how the investment is presented for approval. If one says there is a sure payback of $200,000 for project A or a 50% payback of $400,000 for project B, most people will choose the sure thing because the loss is internalized as a greater loss than the prospect of the gain.

Those people high in *achievement* motive tend to not value losses more than wins, there is a low influence of the Gain/Losses Bias for them. Once again, high achievers see the situation as a rational problem to be solved and are not influenced by other considerations. Also, those high in *personal causation* will experience a low impact of the Gain/Loss Bias since they have a higher reality perception (see Figure 5-3). People high in *affiliation* will show a high impact in the Gain/Losses Bias since they hypothesize the impact on people and the feelings of losing. Also, those high in *power* will be found to have a high impact of the Gains/Losses Bias due to the broad view that considers future options and impact of people. In the house buying story Uncle Leonard is drawn to remodeling to avoid the risk of losing the entire investment all at once. In George's case, he would not be affected by remodeling over having the entire expense of a purchase outright.

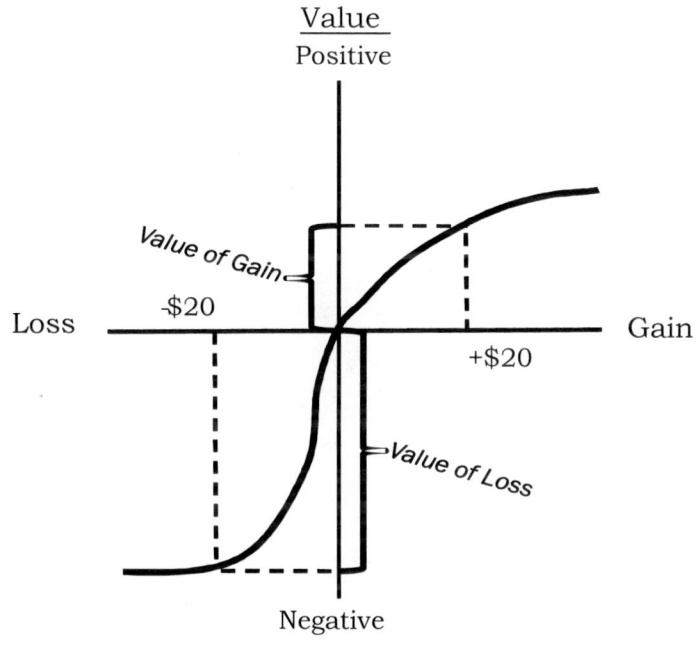

Values of Gains Verses Losses (Heuristics)
Figure 5-2

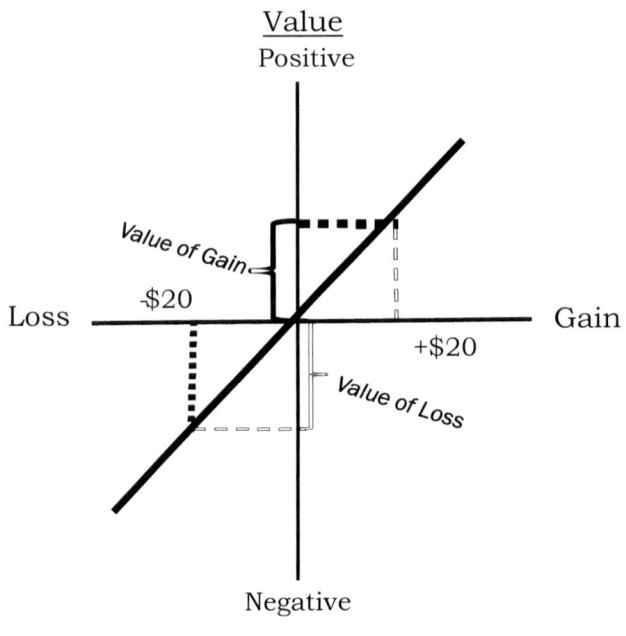

Values of Gains Versus Losses for High in
Achievement and *Personal Causation*
Figure 5-3

Framing Bias – Psychological Accounting (5)

Framing is also identified as sort of psychological accounting, another way of short-cut thinking. Categories of value are inconsistent across instances and people make choices sometimes by these categories because it is easier mentally. Suppose one is going to the theatre and on the way loses the $80 ticket. Would the person buy another ticket with the $100 in their pocket? The framing bias predicts most people would not. But suppose while on the way to the theater, having not purchased the ticket as yet, the person discovers in their pocket that instead of the $180 they had that morning, they now have only $100. They lost $80 in cash. Would the person buy a ticket? The framing bias predicts most people would, though not all. Motives come into play again. Framing as a "problem solving" bias would not have impact of those with *achievement*, and/or *personal causation* motives, they would buy another ticket. And those with *power* and/or *affiliation* would tend to have an influence from the framing bias, and not buy another ticket.

Multi-Tasking Bias (6)

We often think at a different level, or speed, depending on the situation. When multi-tasking, thinking slowly and deliberately for two simultaneous tasks is nearly impossible. We usually switch to a rule-of-thumb quick process for one of the tasks. As an example of this multi-tasking bias, suppose you are driving along at a comfortable rate of speed on autopilot along a road you know well and are engrossed in a debate with your passenger. Your autopilot thinking about driving the car is referred to as system-1 thinking. Your engaging conversation requires deeper thinking, referred to as system-2 thinking. Change the circumstances to a busy interstate highway with many vehicles passing, changing lanes, and speeding, as often is the case, your system-2 is engaged in the driving and you will most likely not hear much of what your passenger is saying. (Let's hope they are not asking you a critical question like "should we get married", and your response is "huh" while you just miss the truck that cut you off.) How you are cognitively engaged in the situation, whether system-1 or system-2, will make a difference on any decision made. People high in the *achievement* motive are less likely to be thinking in system-1 since the world is usually seen as a series of problems to the solved. These people are more likely to recognize the problem of talking in busy traffic, and either not comment at all or suggest the conversation wait until it can be considered more deliberately. Those high in *affiliation* may appear reckless since they may not be attending to busy traffic when someone is conversing with them. Their high need for *affiliation* will draw them to the relationship with the other person and not the traffic. People high in *achievement* may many times be assessed as someone who can only think of one thing at a time, while someone high in *affiliation* may give the appearance of a multi-tasker but often miss a critical piece of a conversation or information to solve a problem. In the house buying story, Whitney, high in *achievement*, put off discussing their options while driving back so she could concentrate on what everyone was thinking.

Thinking Speed Bias (7)

Managers conducting routine status review meetings are usually not expecting nor want a problem-solving session, but just to report status. They would like those involved in the meeting to be engaged in system-1 thinking. To do so the meeting should be easy going, no surprises, in familiar surroundings, with everyone in a good mood. However, some may be led into a system-1 status review process, while others may engage in a system-2 problem-solving process, thus causing some disruption. Be prepared for disruptions when many of those attending are high in the *achievement* motive. Put a problem-solving issue at the end of the status meeting and ask those to stay who wish to work through it. It is important to know who is in attendance in terms of their individual motives.

Someone high in the *power* motive would tend to make these assessments.

When it comes to problem-solving meetings, you would like to engage the attendee's system-2 thinking and need to set up this climate within the meeting venue. People high in *achievement* and *personal causation* motives are ideal for problem solving meetings. New ideas should be encouraged and the meeting environment should be novel and challenging like a retreat atmosphere intended to maximize the stimulation of innovative thought. However, if the retreat is presented as a way for everyone to get to know one another, those high in *personal causation* and *achievement* but low in *affiliation* would tend to avoid it. Those high in *power* and *affiliation* would find such a relationship-style retreat something to anticipate. Someone high in the *power* motive would sense the necessity to pay attention to meeting style and venue since their concern would be the people in order to realize their contribution. In the house buying story Uncle Leonard, high in *power*, was wise in making them come together in a meeting to see how they might collectively resolve the overall problem of buying a house.

Endowment Bias (8)

For most people items that are owned often take on a value that is not reflected by their monetary worth. It is the feeling that the value of something owned is greater than its actual market value. This is sometimes referred to as the status quo bias or regret bias (not wanting to let go of something for fear of future regret), or the endowment bias. In one example a cup with a value of $6.00 is given to several people along with a slip of paper. They are to write on the slip of paper how much they would sell the cup for. Each person with a cup has a counterpart who has been provided a slip of paper, and on this slip the counterpart (or buyer) is asked to write down how much they would pay for the cup. The average purchase price written from the buyers was $2.87 and the average selling price written down by the cups' owners was $7.12. The endowment effect is used to explain what makes a $6.00 cup worth $7.12 if you own it. This same behavior can be seen in automobile prices where the fair market of the automobile seems to always be less than the seller is willing to acknowledge.

The endowment effect was also shown to be in effect for stock portfolio managers. Portfolio managers had a tendency to hold stocks longer than what reasonable stock professionals would advise. In one organization they decided to periodically switch portfolio managers between portfolios. For these managers their portfolios' performances went up. They were no longer held victim to the endowment bias.

An exception to the endowment effect is for those high in the *achievement* motive. These people tended to see things as they actually are – they see it as a problem to be solved and slow their thinking giving it deliberate thought. People high in *affiliation,* while mainly concerned about relationships with people, may tend to be overly influenced by the endowment bias since they might see some sort of personal relationship with what they have. For example, when it was time to buy a better car, I felt my car "Rosy" was certainly worth more than the trade in value I eventually received.

Buying a House Story Reflection

Understanding motives when a group is involved with making decisions can make the process much more efficient as well as more effective. In the house buying story each person approached the problem a bit differently. Yet it worked out in the end due to negotiating through behaviors that are motive driven. The heuristics and biases in Behavioral Economics go a long way in explaining why some people use non-rational processes when choosing. However, the key and root cause for differing ways of choosing lies in the individual motive syndromes of each person.

In the story George and Whitney each approach the house purchase as logical problem to be solved since they both were high in the *achievement* motive. Marie looked at the situation socially due to her high *affiliation* motive and Uncle Leonard saw an opportunity to bring people together and help make the decision due to his high *power* motive. Sometimes in group situations someone high in *power* steps in to coordinate the others to reach an acceptable outcome. However, each person can become aware of the other's motives and negotiate successfully since through this awareness they can balance their own motives with those of the others.

Shared Motives

When it comes to making choices, motives are key for people to come together for mutual benefit. As was evident in the home purchase story, multiple people with differing motives make choices in differing ways. Yet, as was the case, it can result in a positive outcome. Examining the simple interaction between two individuals with the same predominant motive reveals interesting behaviors, some beneficial and some not. We are considering two people sharing the same single predominant motive of *achievement, affiliation, power,* and pers*onal causation* These are syndromes 2 (*achievement*); 6 (*affiliation*); 5 (*power*); and 3 (*personal causation*).

When two people share the predominant motive of *achievement,* it is possible they come to a result of a choice too quickly. This happens when the goals that each person establishes are aligned producing behaviors that are reinforcing, leading to quick conclusions sought by high achievers. You will see them working together quickly to achieve their shared goal. When the goals are not aligned, dispute over goals may result in a lengthy process for choosing or making decisions. The key to these two individuals is to make sure their goals are aligned, yet not be overzealous in goal alignment so that relevant information is missed.

For two people who share the *affiliation* motive, they also may make choices and decisions too quickly. This happens, not because of shared goals, but because of shared values. What each person values could be the same, and the decision will then be based on those values. However, their values may not be the appropriate ones for the entire situation. Therefore, these people need to ensure their values match what the situation calls for. For instance, two people may buy a house because it really feels right, and it suits who they think they are (their values). But after its purchase they may find that meeting the mortgage payments changes their budget reducing other things they would have liked to do, such as international traveling.

When the *power* motive is shared by two individuals, they each have the desire to control the outcome good for the other. They also want to be helpful to the other person in the choice or decision process. Since they share a need to control for the good of the other person, reaching results can produce arguments about how one should go forward. What is needed is to draw boundaries on each person and what they should do to make a mutual decision or a choice that is beneficial for both parties. Arguments about how to reach a good outcome delay making choices or decisions. Those with a shared *power* motive have the danger of delay, that is, they may move too slowly. To overcome this, they need to set boundaries for each other so that they can work on their own part of the decision or choice. As an example, suppose two people plan to buy a car together. The first person wants to go into the car dealership and set up several cars to see and have a preliminary discussion with the salesman in order to make the visit more opportune. The other person also wants to make it easy on the first person contact several dealerships and ask them to set up the best car given their criteria. So, in one case, we have one dealership involved, while in the other, we have multiple dealerships participating. When the day arrives to actually go look for cars, the two people have planned differently for the most productive day to gather information to make a purchase decision. What ensues is usually an argument or dispute on the differing plans. It leads to a non-productive result where no dealership is visited that day. What these *power* people need is to make sure that boundaries are drawn beforehand. For instance, someone could be in charge of setting up dealership visits, and the other could be in charge of organizing the evaluation criteria for the car.

When two people share the *personal causation* motive the result may often be delayed as well. The delay is not over a dispute about who could control what, but on how they could creatively reach a decision. What could result is a never-ending process of how improvements could be made to the process of making a choice or deciding. Each person has the need to be creative and innovative to improve any situation. For instance, partners in a business decide to subcontract the building of another one of their parts used in their product since it is very costly to build it in-house. They have to decide what criteria they use to choose the subcontractor. One person believes they should look at all the people they know who already supply some of their parts at the current time to see what they can possibly do to build this part. During this discussion they figure out some of the parts suppliers have grown so large they may not have capacity to take on another part. They go back to their list and eliminate those. However, after further exploration they realize that some of their own customers are using some subcontractors that they need to avoid because of potential for conflict-of-interest issues. The discussion evolves into consideration for building an operation to produce just that part. That produces the thought that perhaps they could re-engineer the product to do away with that sort of part. With two people high in *personal causation,* they are innovative and produce a never-ending analysis. What is needed are solid deadlines in order to reach a timely conclusion, and actually send out bids for producing the part. For syndromes that have more than one dominate motive, the speeds are usually normal since there is a balance between individuals across the motives.

Next, another story is used to point out how various motive syndromes interact, and at times bring people to a variety of decision outcomes.

144

Murder Story

Malone came into the office at what most people would think would be an awfully late hour. It was raining outside he really didn't care if anybody came in to sit down in his client chair or not. No one should be out this late anyway. Right now, he needed a break because he just completed a tough week on a case where the police concluded the wife killed the husband with a small handgun. Had their conclusion been right or way off? The police, Sergeant McCadden in particular, were like bulls in a China shop. They marched in and started interviewing everyone about what had happened, namely, the wife, Louise; the daughter, Cheryl; the maid, Natasha; and their visiting neighbor, Grace. Sergeant Grayson uses the standard procedure for interviewing witnesses with the added notion that everyone he interviews is a suspect. He gets people so wound up that it is hard to tell whether he is determining what actually happened, what someone thinks actually happened, what someone thinks what someone else thinks happened, a lie, or even a near confession. He is the hammer and everyone else is a nail.

Malone is thinking "I have learned to be nice, polite, and take everyone as they come. Look for not only what they say but how they say it. And what they say about others."

He hears the outside door to his waiting area open and someone obeys the sign "Cindy is out, BE SEATED, with you shortly." After waiting long enough for them to leave if they have had second thoughts about coming in. Then he closes the drawer where he keeps a bottle and pushes himself up off the chair and snails his way over to his door hoping no one will now be there. No luck, it is the visiting neighbor, Grace.

145

"Good evening, Grace, what brings you out on a night like this, I thought you would be home snuggling with your husband."

"Fat chance, he gets home so late it's usually just me and the dog this time of night."

"So, I guess the dog is missing you tonight. Why did you want to see me?"

"It's that neighbor of mine, she thinks she can get away with murder just because her husband was really rich and now, she'll be loaded." Grace said. "I was over there last week and heard them in a real shouting match. They were so loud that I could hear them from my car in the driveway. I think the police are correct in their conclusion and told them so. I'm wondering why you are still looking into the murder. Our neighborhood would be better off if we got rid of that family. I'm here to ask you to end your investigation."

"Louise's daughter, Cheryl, believes her mother is innocent since she sees her as a tender woman who is concerned about everyone's welfare. She asked me to look into it."

"I realize Cheryl is concerned but she needs to adopt a more realistic attitude and see what is obvious," Grace said. "Her parents were never an ideal couple."

At that moment the phone rang and it was Sargent McCadden. Malone put it on speaker so Grace could also hear.

"Malone, I want to speak with you," McCadden shouted over the phone. "What's this I hear about you investigating the Frank murder case. Don't you get it, the wife did it, and there is no more to be gone over. The wife is usually the guilty party in these types of cases. I've got enough on my plate without you dragging this thing out. Grace was just in here and put the nail in the coffin. She heard them arguing, and thought she heard Louise threatening Frank."

"After speaking with Cheryl and the maid, Natasha, it turns out there was no argument at all. In fact, they were planning a second honeymoon trip to Barbados," Malone said. "Cheryl said her dad had many times heard her parents' belief that they were really sole mates, and basically lived for each other's happiness and joy. Natasha expressed a similar idea. McCadden, you really need to hold off judgment until you get all the facts."

"So, since you are such a brainiac, what is your conclusion?" Before Malone could answer McCadden, he heard a rustling and looked up to see Grace standing in front of him pointing a gun at his chest.

"What's with the gun Grace?" Malone said calmly.

With a trembling voice and wild eyes, Grace announced "you're going to tell him I did it. Well, you're right. I did everything to make Frank my lover but with no luck. I'd had it. So, if I can't have him, that woman will not have him either. Malone, if I remove you from this, then I'm in the clear," she said emphasizing each word by the barrel of the gun.

The phone speaker came to life: "Grace, you have no chance now, I heard everything." McCadden said. "Put the gun down and I'll come over."

Her guilt revealed she could no longer stand the pressure and handed the gun to Malone and then collapsed in the chair.

Murder Story Reflection

In the story we see people making choices from different syndromes. Sergeant McCadden is high in *achievement* and high in *personal causation*. McCadden is quick to arrive at a conclusion indicative of his reaching a goal under his own purview. Malone is a contrast to McCadden. He is high in *affiliation* and *power*. He looks at the situation with the people in mind and tries to control the outcome to everyone's satisfaction (except Grace). Grace is aware of the impact of her decision on people, but will use her own creativity to satisfy what she thinks others value (except Malone).

Motives and Choices Reflection

People use different ways of choosing as a function of their motives. We can see that the basis of choices are really motives, but there are other complicating factors that need to be taken into account. One complicating factor are the eight heuristics and biases people have about choices as highlighted by Behavioral Economics. Another complicating factor for choosing are the motives of others involved in the decision. People working together either one-on-one, or with a group may find that their respective motives confirm the choosing process, or sometimes set the stage for disputes that could lead to delays as could have been the case in the murder story.

Chapter 6

Motive Syndromes and Group Identity

Let them eat cake

Marie-Antoinette

Group motive syndromes are indicators of the kinds of groups that individuals prefer as well as how groups differ in their behaviors and expectations. A boy scout group will function differently from a surgical group, and the people who are most comfortable in one will likely not be comfortable in the other. It is just not a question of age, but of key expectations of the group, and how people in the group expect to interact. The basis for group identity is a social process that has its foundation in the motives of individuals in the group. While some motives rank low or medium, a high motive strength in one or two of the motives of achi*evement, affiliation, power,* and/or *person causation* furnishes that foundation.

Group Formation and Identity

Groups have their own identity and function in ways that at times seem unreasonable or illogical. The group identity is a social norm and has an impact on making decisions just as seen with Behavioral Economics (see Chapter 5). Three factors are important for developing group identity. One is shared experience(s). When a large collection of people share experiences deeply and over long periods of time a culture begins to form. The same phenomenon is true of any group. Groups form their own culture. Before a culture sets in, a group begins to develop a sense of identity that starts from shared experience(s). Shared experience(s) is step one in forming group identity.

The second factor in forming group identity is to share a primary belief or a fundamental way of understanding the world – a common worldview. The worldview does not need to be a complete set of attitudes or beliefs, but a main element with which each member can identify. It may be a common goal, a common enemy, or even the sense of a common threat. For example, a story circulated about a group of software testers working at IBM. Everyone disliked them, which lead to finding people to participate as members of the testing group no easy task. Once the group fully grasped that they shared a common belief of protector of quality, they began to act as a cohesive group with their own identity. They dressed in black and began to achieve a reputation throughout the organization as tough people.

The third factor in forming group identity is a sense of closure. Closure occurs when a task or effort results in a completion – a sense of "doneness." The shared experience of closure provides a sense of group accomplishment and the opportunity to realize "we couldn't have done it without you". This phrase applies to each member of the group, so that what is really shared is a sense of one another's value to the whole. Each time a music rehearsal is concluded, the musicians have the opportunity to feel a sense of closure. Even though the job is not done there is a sense of having completed a step within an overall process. To summarize the elements in the formation of group identity:

1. Shared experience(s)
2. Shared belief(s)
3. Sense of closure

An example of group identity is found in the impact of war on soldiers. Indoctrination into the armed forces, either through boot camp or other training, introduces a common worldview and provides an initial experience of closure. Additional closures were experienced at every conclusion of an encounter with the enemy, or completion of significant training exercises. Shared experiences; primary belief (common enemy, or pride in being able to serve); and experienced closure, created high levels of group identity. In some cases, their group identity remained well into their future lives.

What becomes natural group behavior is a byproduct of the motive syndrome that predominantly supports the group's formation factors especially shared beliefs. In the case of the wartime soldiers the motives are *achievement* and *affiliation* (identified below as a Candid motive syndrome). Soldiers are highly dependent on one another sparking a high *affiliation* motive; however, they must accomplish goals to sustain the group which engages the *achievement* motive.

Groups with different shared beliefs engage motives differently as a result they carry out their group behaviors in ways that differ. These taken-for-granted behaviors are most evident to the individuals who first join an existing group. They feel there is something going on they do not understand. The assumptions that the group relies on are not made explicit. If one joins a group, the assumptions become implicit over time; that is, they can be adopted without explicit training by participating in the activities of the group. Beliefs can build through an indoctrination process by using a series of exercises or on-the-job training assignments.

Motive Syndromes and the Formation of Group Identity

Group identity finds its basis in motives. Group motive syndromes are identified with one or two predominant, or high, motives. If there are one or two predominant motive syndromes within a group those syndromes will act as formative agents in how the group comes together to function. The force that forms a group needs the strength of at least one or two motives. Ten group motive syndromes are possible from the four motives of *achievement, affiliation, power,* and *personal causation.* These group forming motive syndromes are based on how members of the group interact.

1. Insistent - Get it right no matter what
2. Immediacy - Get it done now
3. Creative - Get it done creatively
4. Sensitive - Consider all sensitivities
5. Influential - Delicately influence
6. Moral - Adjust to values
7. Candid - Push through sensitivities
8. Tactful - Work around sensitivities
9. Controlling - Influence to a result
10. Performative – Strict reality influence

The predominant motives that form these syndromes are shown in Figure 6-1. The predominate, or "High", motives are identified in the figure.

Group Syndromes		Motives			
		Ach	Affil	Pow	Pers Causa
1	Insistent	High			High
2	Immediate	High			
3	Creative				High
4	Sensitive		High	High	
5	Influential			High	
6	Moral		High		
7	Candid	High	High		
8	Tactful		High		High
9	Controlling	High		High	
10	Performative			High	High

Figure 6-1
Group Motive Syndromes

Insistent Group Syndrome (1)

These groups are high in the *achievement* motive in order to meet their intended goals, plus high in the *personal causation* motive by being innovative and creative in these goal pursuits. "Get it right no matter what." We can use this motto for an insistent kind of group. The group finds its identity by accomplishing specific goals and uses any means they can to a realize these goals. Results can be very creative and at times very pleasing to others. We see this in outstanding orchestras that have as their goal perfection in performance, with each member listening and adding their part to produce a creative mix of sound as they reach for perfection.

On the other hand, insistent groups may seek accomplishment of their personal goals through what they see as boundaryless freedom. Biker gangs such as Hell's Angels, are examples of this kind of group. They may see their freedom to be disruptive to others as one way to reach their goal of being social outcasts in any way possible.

Immediacy Group Syndrome (2)

The immediacy group syndrome is high in the *achievement* motive but medium or low in the *affiliation, power,* and *personal causation* motives. Groups with this syndrome are primarily concerned with accomplishing the goal, and may be characterized as "Get it done now." The professional preseason sports camp/tryout is a good example of this syndrome. Reaching the goals such as speed, accuracy, or endurance is the ultimate test of the athletes. They are not there to make friends or be creative, but to show what they can do now.

Another example of the immediacy group syndrome is an automobile racing team pit crew. While their relationships (*affiliation* motive) seem important, they are ultimately judged on their speed and accuracy for getting the automobile in and out of the pit quickly. There may have been some creativity (*personal causation* motive) in designing their process, but once designed the performance to goal achievement is what really counts.

Creative Group Syndrome (3)

Creative group syndrome is primarily governed by the *personal causation* motive. The other motives of *achievement, affiliation,* and *power* are not that important; they would be medium or low. "Get it done creatively" is a motto for groups with this syndrome. A jazz trio is an example of this. They are not committed to following a particular music score, nor do they set out to produce any one particular sound, as a group with an *achievement* motive would. The group may be friends, as in the *affiliation* motive, and want each other to succeed, as in the *power* motive, but the group is primarily driven by their need to collaborate creatively in a performance. *Personal causation* is indeed the driving force of this kind of group.

Another example of this kind of group would be a group of collaborators brought together to write a new stage play. Their main focus is to come up with ideas for a storyline and get them "down on paper." The *achievement* motive could play into this as well because they have a goal to reach, but the group is primarily formed to create a manuscript, which takes precedence over all other things.

The GNU Project, a computer software endeavor, is another example of the creative group syndrome. This effort is dedicated to collaboration and creativity for computer software systems design, building, and usage. The result of the effort is free software that supplants the fees associated with other computer systems software such as Windows. The most famous outcome of the project is the Linux operating system, along with all its add-on functionalities. This group builds free software and is primarily concerned with creative useful results, as is true for people high in the *personal causation* motive.

155

Sensitive Group Syndrome (4)

The Sensitive motive syndrome is all about caring for others as a goal, organizing activities and events to produce preferred ideals, and being sensitive to values This syndrome is associated with high *affiliation* and high *power* motives. Group identity forms around a concern for people, both for fiends, as in the *affiliation* motive; and for the current and future welfare of people, as in the *power* motive.

This syndrome represents an overall concern for the welfare of other people. People with this syndrome are concerned with making friends, as well as the success of current and future life position of others. They are the ones others often go to for advice and, unfortunately, often give advice when it is not requested. They go out of their way to be helpful in personal and professional relationships. We see this behavior in many religious groups, particularly in Christian-oriented groups. Common admonitions are turn the other cheek, love your enemies, do not judge others, go the extra mile, the golden rule, and do unto others as you would have them do unto you. Groups that have these sorts of ideals are the American Red Cross, many hospitals, orphanages, and homeless shelters.

Influential Group Syndrome (5)

This motive syndrome is indicative of a high *power* motive. This kind of power concerns an individual's welfare as a life position and not as in a friendship. High school or college subject-oriented study groups are suited to this syndrome. They are concerned with being excellent in their study and not becoming close friends. While friendships could ensue, it is not the point of the study. If friendships become as important, the goal of becoming better at the subject may even suffer. Another example would be therapy groups which primarily targeting the well-being of others and do not building friendships.

Moral Group Syndrome (6)

This syndrome is focused on the *affiliation* motive. These groups rely primarily on establishing, growing, or maintaining relationships. Concentration is on social mores and norms of the group. A friendship clique is an example of this syndrome. People are not concerned about controlling interactions for the good of their current or future welfare, as in the *power* motive; nor about accomplishing some goal, as in the *achievement* motive; nor concerning being creative, and in the *personal causation* motive. Barriers into these groups are hard to cross, yet the barriers can be torn down if the group's set of assumptions about the world have been shown to be false.

Years ago, an elementary teacher, trying to explain to her students the idea of prejudice in the wake of Martin Luther King's assassination, told her class if they wanted to learn prejudice, she had something for them to do as an exercise. Blue-eyed children were set apart from the children with brown eyes. Green construction paper armbands were to be worn by the blue-eyed kids. She told the class the brown-eyed kids were better people, cleaner and more intelligent. She described blue-eyed kids as being lazy and, if given something to do, they would mess it up. She made the blue-eyed kids drink from cups at the water fountain so as not to contaminate the water for the brown-eyed kids. It was not long before the brown-eyed kids began to treat the blue-eyed kids rather badly, by putting them down and making them feel inferior, both in the classroom and at recess. The following week she reversed the roles in which the blue-eyed kids were considered more important than the brown-eyed, and the behavior changed so that the brown-eyed kids were now put-down by the blue-eyed kids. When the kids were asked after the exercise was over to write down how they felt, the brown-eyed kids said they felt like hitting the blue-eyed kids since they were so inferior. However, when the roles were reversed the brown-eyed kids said they were mad and wanted to quit school. Upon reflection the kids saw what it was like to be prejudiced and were happy to have had the exercise.

While the exercise certainly revealed how easy and forceful prejudice can find its way into groups, it also shows that social identity of a group is easily formed and that group identity can come from the simplest of ideas. The primary group identity consists of experienced social norms based on the *affiliation* motive. Their behavior was wrapped up in how they related to each other socially. Groups so formed see the basis for interacting as a moral position. The "other-eyed" children were assumed not to measure up in some way, namely, a moral position based on shared values of the group. The way group members treat each other along with how they treat other people is founded on engagement of the *affiliation* motive. If a group's identity is formed primarily in a social way, then activities and opinions rely on morally-based criteria.

In a similar example, some groups develop an identity that considers their competition less able and even less moral. Early in his presidency John F. Kennedy decided something needed to be done with Cuba since it was communist, associated with the Soviet Union, and lay just a few miles off the coast of Florida. He called his cabinet together, a group of very intelligent people, and considered what action if any should be taken. They concluded to invade Cuba at the Bay of Pigs with expatriates of Cuba. The invaders were captured as soon as they reached the shore. In hindsight it was an awful decision, yet made with very intelligent people. Their group identity was formed as one would form a club or friendship clique with a strong leader. Because of this they failed to make a wise decision as would be appropriate for a global super-power. Such decision-making processes have been referred to as Groupthink. Groupthink is characterized by examining few alternatives, not being critical of each other's ideas, not seeking expert opinion, being highly selective in gathering information, not having contingency plans, succumbing to stereotypes which guide the decision, and a strong sense of the group's morality or right to do what they deem best. The cabinet at that time acted more like a clique than a wise counsel to the president. Motives are once again at play in creating such a group identity. Their desire for close relationship, *affiliation* motive, negated other behaviors such as setting and overcoming goals, *achievement* motive, being creative, as in *personal causation* motive, and a concern for the welfare of others, as in the *power* motive.

Candid Group Syndrome (7)

In this group syndrome one sees a high concern for meeting and overcoming goals, as in the *achievement* motives, as well as a concern for building friendships, as in the *affiliation* motive. In an experiment, twenty-two, eleven-year-old boys attended a remote summer camp and were randomly divided into two groups. The boys developed an attachment to their groups during the first week of camp by hiking and swimming. They chose names for their groups, The Eagles and The Rattlers. During a series of competitions involving sport games between the groups, physical and verbal prejudices started.

While in a cooling off period, they commented on features of the two groups. They described their own in-group using very favorable terms, and the other out-group with very unfavorable terms. Then they forced the groups to work together to reach common goals which eased the prejudice and tension among them. Group conflict can result when separate group identities are formed, where the identities are established through competitive activities as in playing sports games against one another. Often referred to as an in-group/out-group situation. One group sees itself as superior to the other group with no real basis for such an attitude. Motives are the basis for the formation of such group identities. For the boy's camp example, the group identity was formed as a combination of social norms and achieving wins in sports activities. They were candid with each other in order to meet their challenges. Deciding who was best to play what position in the sports events, along with which boys became de facto leaders was founded on a combination of the *achievement* motive and the *affiliation* motive. Groups with this identity are sometimes looked on as members being open and truthful, and at times brutally honest.

Winning professional sports teams claim to have developed a spirit that sustains them through hard practices and difficult schedules. Their efforts are made more difficult by balancing family and other commitments that tend to erode attention to the team effort. The team spirit does not develop until the team starts winning. The wins bring closure to their effort, this with their history of practices, performance in other games, along with the goal of winning brings about their group identity. As the famous John Madden said: "I've always said winning's the great deodorant, and conversely, when you have a bad record — everything stinks — and everything starts to unravel, and everything falls apart." The identity of the group becomes clouded and lost when there is insufficient closure brought about by wins. Their shared or primary belief is winning, and this shared belief comes from the motives held by the individuals on the team. Successful professional sports teams have the same notion of group identity as the boy's camp example. They too are concerned with winning, along with working together as a team to form a team spirit. The Candid motive syndrome requires the *achievement* motive as well as the *affiliation* motive to be engaged.

Tactful Group Syndrome (8)

This group motive syndrome is concerned with friendships, as in the *affiliation* motive, as well as creativity/innovation, as in the *personal causation* motive. Of minor importance is overcoming goals, as in the *achievement* motive, or interacting for the welfare of others, as in the *power* motive. Fraternities and sororities are good examples of this group syndrome. They seek others in creative ways as in *personal causation* to build and sustain relationships throughout their college career and beyond. The Moose Lodge is another example of this motive syndrome. Once again, in creative ways as in p*ersonal causation*, they seek out other people to initiate and sustain friendships in keeping with the *affiliation* motive.

Controlling Group Syndrome (9)

In this group motive syndrome, there is a high concern for meeting and perhaps surpassing goals as in the *achievement* motive, along with a high concern for the current and future welfare of others, as in the *power* motive. The surgical team is a good example of this group syndrome. The surgical team is primarily concerned with the health and outcome of their procedure on the patient. Along with this they are not only concerned with achieving an outcome, but an outcome that will be very beneficial to the patient. The two motives of *achievement* and *power* are primary in this motive syndrome. The other motives of *personal causation* and *affiliation* are not high in this group motive syndrome. Surgical teams are not there to be inventive as in the *personal causation* motive or to build a lasting relationship with the patient, as with the *affiliation* motive. Other medical procedural groups, such as dental groups, have the same group motive syndrome: a primary concern for achieving results, along with concern for current and future welfare of their patients.

Performative Group Syndrome (10)

This group syndrome is characterized by a high concern for *power* along with a high concern for *personal causation*. Groups with this syndrome are seeking creative ways for people to have improved current and future welfare. A theatrical troupe is a good example of this group motive syndrome. People in this group are concerned with being creative, yet maintaining a formal relationship with other actors in the performance of their parts. Each actor upholds a part in the play to sustain the story. This requires actors to consider the other person and their current and future place, as in the *power* motive. Yet to be convincing these actors need to be creative in performing their roles, as in the *personal causation* motive. The troupe is not about making and building friendships, as in the *affiliation* motive, nor about simply delivering the lines of the play, as in the *achievement* motive. While memorization is important to the performance of the play it is not the primary concern of the theatrical troupe. The actors sustain the plot of the play by interacting with each other in ways that are often creative; as in instances, someone forgets a line, the stage lighting is incorrect, or the audience is located in untraditional places.

The Event Organizers is another example of this group motive syndrome. In this situation organizers are primarily concerned with how their creativity, as in the *personal causation* motive, can be used to produce a great event. They also want to create something that will benefit those attending which is an example of the presence of the *power* motive.

Membership in Many Groups

If a group has been together long enough to form an identity, members will interact with each other, and to those outside the group, through a learned set of motives developing a group motive syndrome. In some ways we could say the group arouses a set of motives that reinforce the way they go about interacting. Group motive syndromes engaged by individuals in one group, may differ as they move to another group since group identities tend to differ. The natural actions of an individual will usually differ from those in a church or religious group as they move to a sports team.

Overall, an individual is usually a participant in many groups but may find one group easier to belong to than another. This can be attributed to their natural motives that are aligned with the group motive syndrome.

Group Peculiar Features

Behavioral peculiarities arise when groups perform. A group acts in ways that may defy what any individual in the group would do in a given circumstance. These group-specific behaviors include Groupthink (as mentioned previously in the Moral group syndrome); in-group/out-group thinking (as mentioned in the Candid group syndrome); social facilitation; and shirking among others.

Social Facilitation

Social facilitation occurs when the mere presence of the group facilitates the dominant behavior of its members. When a member of the group is performing a routine task the presence of the group will facilitate its performance – the member performs it faster since the dominant response is the actual performance itself. If I am splitting wood logs and the neighbors come over to watch, I will tend to split the wood faster. If I am trying to solve a difficult problem, when colleagues come in to watch, it will take longer to solve the problem since the dominant response is to make mistakes while coming up with a good solution. For well-learned tasks an audience will produce the dominant response which would be a high level of task performance. When the task is being learned, the presence of an audience will degrade the performance, since the dominant response to learning is to make mistakes. This is why a professional musician performs better with an audience, while the amateur tends to do better when practicing alone. These behaviors find their basis in the motives of the individuals. Individual dominant behavior changes when a group identity is formed; individual motive syndromes are replaced by a group motive syndrome leading to individual behaviors in a group that may be different when the individuals are separated from the group, or when they move from one group to another. What behavior becomes dominant for the group is often initiated by the leader, or those who maintain a higher social status in the group. Those in the group that do not individually have the group motive syndrome will find themselves responding differently within the group.

The dominant response when there is no group identity is for individual motive syndromes to arise in the group, often reducing group effectiveness. When the group is well-formed and has developed an identity, the group motive syndrome becomes the dominant motive syndrome for members of the group. As an example, a member of a group that has formed an identity around moral or value-based behaviors, as with the *affiliation* motive, will be affective with these behaviors even though that member individually may be more concerned with immediate results to meet specific goals, as in the *achievement* motive. When a group has formed an identity, the motive basis for that identity has an overwhelming impact on the behavior of group members to the extent that the group motive syndrome overtakes individual motive syndromes.

Shirking

When someone is added to an existing group, the amount of energy that person gives to the group sometimes does not measure up to the energy the existing members are giving. They are shirking their duties. The existing members are accustomed to each other and know how to judge their relative contributions. The new member may often not know how to go about engaging with the group in an equitable way, and may sit back and not participate as much as expected.

The impression of shirking occurs particularly when the groups have an *achievement* motive where there is goal-directed behavior. It has been shown when individuals are asked to rate their relative contribution to the performance of the group, the result, when added together, is often much more than 100%. That is, each individual may see their contribution to the group as being more than other members. This can tend to be true if there is a new member. When members claim their overall contribution is higher than the reality, it supports the notion that other members are shirking some of their duties to the group.

Groups that have formed a strong identity do not usually have any significant shirking taking place. They have learned to communicate openly about their relative contributions, and have found ways to negotiate apparent differences.

Participating in Groups

After a group has formed an identity, the members of the group check their contribution to the group at various times. These times include when someone new joins the group, when new circumstances arise that impact the group, as well as when a key group member leaves the group. Two notions are at work when any of these occur, along with a single predominant motive. One notion is the equity felt by group members, and the other notion is the capacity for members to realize their own Behavior Potential. Equity is a social phenomenon and someone possessing a high degree of the *affiliation* motive or a high degree of the *power* motive would be most affected by a sense of equity in the group. People high in the *achievement* motive or the *personal causation* motive would be most impacted by the opportunities to realize their full Behavior Potential. Achievers want to create and realize goals and those high in *personal causation* are looking to make a creative impact on their world.

There are three forms of equity. One deals with how equitable a situation is between the people who are in it. An example of this form of equity is when you spend many hours, while others spend just a few, building a set for the school play where everyone's children are performing equal parts. Another example is when you observe someone in your English class who always get an A+ for their one-page themes, while you get only a B on your five-page themes that you have had proofread by your college professor uncle who teaches English literature. Inequity occurs for people when someone unfairly is held out as deserving more for their equal contribution to the group than everyone else, or when someone looks like they are getting preferential treatment within the group. Those high in *affiliation* and *power* are much more attuned to their social situation and will tend to make judgments based on equitable positions

Another form of equity is between people in one situation compared with people in a similar situation within the same overall environment. An example of this form of equity can occur between two departments in a business organization. Salespeople in one department work hard to sell their product but receive a higher commission than that of a sister department for the same level or work. The inequity between departments can produce an overall reduction in performance due to time wasted on continual comparisons and voiced justifications as well as displeasures. As another example often in large cities, certain neighborhoods get more attention when it comes to trash collection than others. There may be many reasons for this but whatever they are, those who live in the less served neighborhoods certainly feel that there is an inequity since they are assessed with the same tax rates as the better-served neighborhoods. Much wasted effort can result due to city governments that have to contend with displeased citizenry, as well as those citizens that argue that their neighborhoods should be served better since they are cleaner in general.

A third form of equity is an overall sense of one's contribution that matches what is deemed fair in the world at large. One example of this form of equity is when someone serves in their country's military. They put their life on the line for the good of their country, and upon their return from service, they are honored by the general population. Another example is when a business organization uses profit sharing with their employees. When the business does well, the employees do well which makes it an equitable situation. This does not happen when employees work extra hard to save a business yet do not enjoy the benefits of that extra hard work because all the profits are passed along to senior people or stockholders. This sort of inequity will eventually degrade business performance so that the business survival could be in jeopardy.

With equity, whether it is each member of a group with the others, or one group compared with another, or a group's situation with an overall population, people high in *affiliation* and *personal causation* will be more attuned to these forms of equity. Their sensitivities to inequities can be addressed by balancing their relative contributions.

Members of a group can be more sensitized to realizing their Behavior Potential when these members are high in *achievement* or high in *personal causation*. In groups the abilities and knowledge of members match the opportunities presented to the group, accomplishment as in achieving an outcome, and creativity as in initiating activities, are driving forces of the group. (See previous examples of pre-season sports camp, jazz group, and pit crew.) Members are driven to realize their own individual contributions, and equity is not that important to them.

Motives in Your Life

Chapter 7

Overall Analysis – Putting it Together

No one can make you feel inferior without your consent   Eleanor Roosevelt

Motives play an important part in life. By analyzing one's natural and cognitive motives and reflecting on how motives impact changes in life circumstances, it may be possible to improve one's way of living. Changes in life circumstances (e.g., new job, relocation, divorce, retirement, and more) can be more effectively accommodated by knowing your motives and the motive climates that are inherent in these circumstances. By comparing natural motives with cognitive motives, one can get a sense of what comes naturally to a person versus what they think would be natural for oneself. The cognitive motive assessment reveals how one thinks about oneself while the natural motive assessment reveals a natural tendency to act. The natural motive assessment reveals one's internal energy for initiating behaviors and is key to understanding how one lives in one's environment.

Comparative Motive Analysis Chart

A Comparative Motive Analysis (CMA) Chart, shown below in Figure 7-1, compares your cognitive motive assessment, with what you think are your motives, with your natural motive assessment, and with what are really your motives. Cognitive and natural scores for each of the four motives are placed on the chart and provide a visual representation of their relative strength, and can be used as an aid for analyzing motives. Cognitive scores come from question/answer assessments, while natural scores come from story assessments

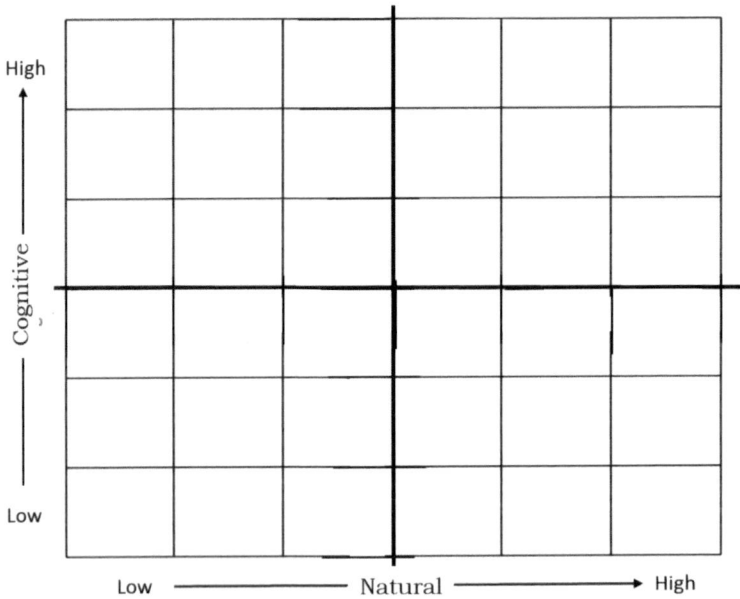

Figure 7-1
Comparative Motive Analysis (CMA) Chart

Any motive data point shown above the middle horizontal line is higher than the cognitive average, while below it is lower than cognitive average. Any motive data point to the right of the vertical dividing line is higher than the natural motive average and to the left it is lower. The chart contains four data points, one for each of the four motives of *achievement affiliation, power*, and *personal causation*. A data point represents both the natural and cognitive scores. Averages have come from hundreds of assessments taken over 10 years of over 200 subjects. When someone is higher in their cognitive motive score than their natural, they think they have more of a motive than they really do. They should not be encouraged to engage in opportunities best suited for that motive. However motive training and understanding would be a possible remedy to satisfy and develop the perceived motive (see Appendix 2 and Chapter 2 for motive training). The *achievement* motive in Figure 7-2 is an example of this. When your motive scores higher in natural motive than your cognitive, then you have more of a motive than you are aware, and should be coached to engage more with that motive in life's various opportunities. The *affiliation* motive is an example of this in Figure 7-2. The data points for *power* and *personal causation* motives in Figure 7-2 are both medium (average ratings).

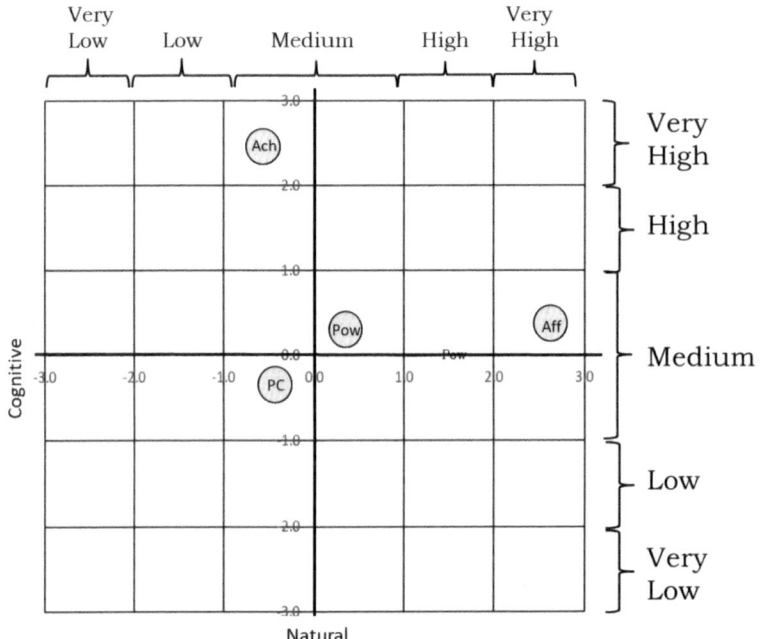

Figure 7-2
Comparative Motive Analysis Chart
With Example Data Points

Assessment Options

Assessments can be made at several levels of accuracy. The most accurate assessment is done by pa professional as through Albers Adams Institute. The next level is by your personal use of an accompany workbook that provides examples and scoring instructions. A quicker and easier, but less accurate, method would be to use the Short Motive Assessment as shown in Appendix 1 (see Figure 7-3).

Motive Assessments	Estimated Accuracy
Professional Version Alberts Adams Institute*	Extremely
Advanced Version Workbook	Highly
Short Version Appendix 2	Medium

* albertsadamsllc@gmail.com

Figure 7-3
Natural and Cognitive Motive
Assessments Options

Following is another example of results as developed using the Short Motive Assessment. While the Comparative Motive Chart is presented in the same way, the results are less accurate but still useful. From the Comparative Motive Chart in Figure 7-4 with the accompanying summary in Figure 7-5.

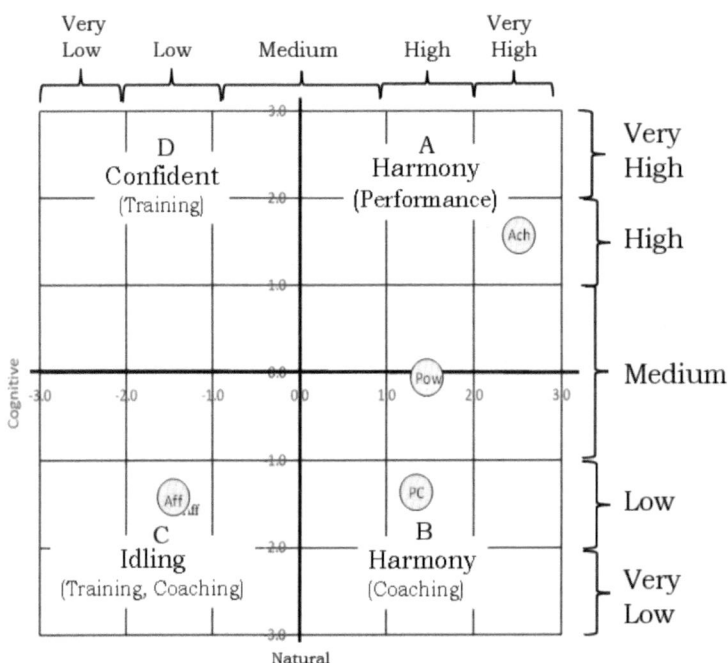

Figure 7-4
Comparative Motive Analysis Chart with Table Data

　　Data in Figure 7-4 and the Comparative Motive Analysis Chart in Figure 7-5 show an individual who is Very High in the natural *achievement* motive, this is the raw score and the transformed score) and High in the cognitive assessment of the *achievement* motive. It also shows a score greater in the natural *power* motive than their cognitive assessment of *power*. The person has more *power* motive than they know. The same is true of their *personal causation* motive. It is scored higher naturally than cognitively. The *affiliation* motive is scored Low naturally and cognitively. Based on the person's scores as seen on the chart, the person would not take on activities that are *affiliation* oriented, as they would probably tend to take on activities that are *achievement* oriented, but could take on even more. Also, the person would probably be hesitant to take on activities that actually would be natural for their *power* capability.

Motive Syndromes Analysis

Figure 7-5 displays the motives and the various Motive Syndromes (presented in earlier chapters) on one master sheet. The data suggests this person is highest in *achievement* and *power* motives (while *personal causation* is High naturally, but since it is Low cognitively, it would take some coaching to bring it into awareness). The data indicates the person is a natural Doer. However, with at least one strong motive present in *achievement,* they could be a near natural Overcomer or Actioner personality. With a High *power* motive, the person could be a near natural Agent or Dominator personality.

Syndromes / Motives	Assessment Data	Doer	Overcomer	Agent	Actioner	Dominator
General Chapter 1		Doer	Overcomer	Agent	Actioner	Dominator
Classic Trait Behavior Chapter 2		Melancholic	Phlegmatic	NA	NA	NA
Leadership Chapter 3		Mover	Innovator	NA	NA	NA
Careers Chapter 4		Directing	Initiating	Leading	Directing Somewhat	Directing Somewhat
Choices Chapter 5		Influence to a Result	Get it Right no Matter	Reality Influence	Get it Done	Sensitively Influence
Groups Chapter 6		Controlling	Insistent	Performance	Immediate	Influential
Achievement	Nat. – Very High Cogni. - High	High	High		High	
Affiliation	Nat.- Low Cogni. - Low					
Power	Nat. High Cogni. - Medium	High	High	High		High
Personal Causation	Nat. - High Cogni. - Low			High	High	

Figure 7-5
Natural Motive Syndromes Summary

This person would benefit from being engaged in *achievement* opportunities. With their natural *power* motive, this person should be counseled to take up leadership positions that require a Mover, since a Mover is High in *achievement* and High in *power* motives. This person is someone who gets things done by engaging other people to everyone's benefit. Their motives fit careers involved with controlling, such as, project manager, business department manager, specializing medical doctor, airline pilot captain, or managing editor. They would be ill-suited for careers with mutuality needs, such as, investment counseling, account executive, minister, alumni development specialist, management of a large benevolent enterprise, field representative, or someone in sustained sales (see Chapter 4).

Motive Counseling with Careers

Comparative Motive Analysis can reveal one's naturally best motives, as well as identifying 'motive conflict' problems when someone thinks they have a motive but really does not. If someone wants a career that does not fit their natural motives, yet incorrectly think they have the relevant motives, they should be advised to get motive training to increase what they lack. If examination of someone's Comparative Motive Analysis chart shows they have natural motive(s) for which they are unaware, they should be coached to investigate careers that fit those motive(s).

The Comparative Motive Analysis chart provides a visual determination of the need for training or coaching. If the motive needs to be moved to the right in the chart, then training is needed. If the motive needs to move up in the chart, coaching is needed. A motive is trained over, and coached up. (See Figure 7-6.)

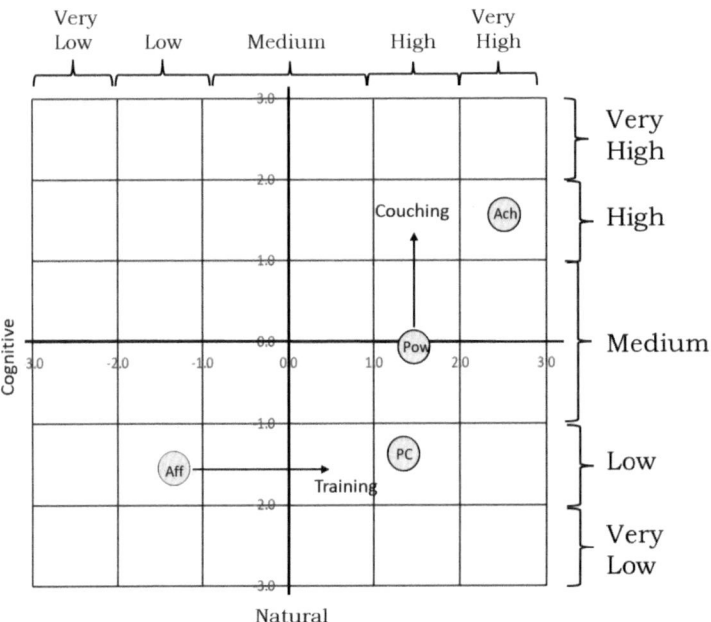

Figure 7-6
Comparative Motive Analysis Chart Training and
Coaching Application

The good news is that Comparative Motive Analysis may confirm one's career choice when motives align with career motives, or validate their feeling that their career is not self-rewarding when motives are conflicted. Also, after being in a career for several years, it may be a good idea to reexamine motives using these assessments and analysis tools. A career may turn out to be different than expected due to both circumstances and the people involved in the career. Natural motives can change given opportunities in the environment, and cognitive motives (self-perception) can change as well due to influences around them. Motives are stable as a rule, but are susceptible to change as life unfolds.

Life Changes and Motives

A good time to examine your motives is when you go through a life changing experience. These can include almost any significant change or interruption in your life. Examples are changing jobs, moving locations, retiring, and many others. The following is a quick review of those changes to provide an insight of how you can examine such changes in your life.

Changing Jobs

When changing jobs, it is a good idea to reexamine your current motives and the motives that were important in your old job as compared to motives that are important in your new job. Often if you are changing jobs within the same company, these motives changes are probably going to be minor since both jobs are within the same company culture. When changing to a similar job from one company that is somewhat like the company you are leaving, the motives will probably be fairly consistent between the companies. When moving from a current job to a new job where the company has different assumptions about how people work, then a motives examination would be valuable in order to engage comfortably and productively with the new job. First examine the organizational cultures (see Chapter 3, and Figure 7-9 below), then determine how your current motives fit the cultures.

If you are moving to a company culture that is *achievement* oriented; and is managed with an implicit *power* motive (Target culture); and you are leaving a Familial/Clan culture (High in *affiliation* and *personal causation*) that fits you well, you should expect some difficulty fitting into the new job. You would be uncomfortable with the required organizational demands that a *power* culture has, and the expected drive and goal setting nature that an *achievement* culture expects. Motives analysis would give you the information to determine whether your natural motives would be in line with the new job. If not, then it would be beneficial for you to get training (See Appendix 2 and Chapter 2) or coaching in the motives that are needed. If you are moving from a Familial/Clan culture to a Target culture, you would have to determine whether your natural *achievement* and *power* motives are a good fit. And, if not, then examine your *achievement* and *power* motives and get trained in these motives if necessary. Changing from a Target culture to an Ordered culture, your *affiliation* demands will go up, requiring you to put more value on your relationships. In changing from an Ordered culture to a Target culture means that more *achievement* behaviors would be expected. People with a High *achievement* motive are good at setting goals and striving to meet them which you may not be comfortable with if your *achievement* motive is not High (in the Ordered culture the *affiliation* motive is needed, not the *achievement* motive). If the change would be to move from a Target to an Entrepreneurial culture, more initiative behaviors would be expected as found in the *personal causation* motive. Also, a reliance on organizing which is found in the *power* motive would decrease; control would be replaced with creativity and innovation. In moving from Entrepreneurial to Familial/Clan *affiliation,* behavioral expectations would increase. In moving from Familial/Clan to Entrepreneurial *achievement* behavioral expectations would increase. In moving from Entrepreneurial to Familial/Clan *affiliation* behavioral expectations would increase. In moving from Ordered to Familial/Clan *personal causation* behavioral expectations would increase, and in moving from Familial/Clan to Ordered the *power* motive behavioral expectations would be deemed more important. Finally, in moving from Entrepreneurial to Target the need for understanding *power* behavioral expectations would increase (see Figure 7-7).

Culture Focus

	External *Achievement*	**Internal** *Affiliation*
High *Power*	TARGET	ORDERED
Lower *Personal Causation*	ENTREPRENEURIAL	FAMILIAL/CLAN

Culture Control

Figure 7-7
Organizational Cultures

Changing Locations

Changing locations involves moving from one place to another. The examples provided below represent moving from an urban area (large city, small city) to or from a rural area (farm, settlement, or small town). An examination of the four motives suggests that moving from one location to another will bring differing expectations. Figure 7-8 describes the predominant motives of each of these locations, and are explained below. These predominant motives do not represent personal motives, but a Motive Climate. These are assumptions that the population in each Motive Climate has what is important and what people should naturally want in their lives. No population, whatever the Motive Climate, is homogeneous. Therefore, in each of the Motive Climates, you will find individuals who match your natural wants irrespective of the Motive Climate itself. Often people will gather in sub-climates within the overall Motive Climate to maintain identity for what they feel should be important (see Chapter 6). So, when you are moving from one kind of location to another, it is useful to be aware that its Motive Climate can make the transition smoother and less stressful since you are aware of the expectations.

Location Motive Climate	Predominant Motives within Motive Climate	Behaviors within Motive Climate
Large City Climate Urban 1	Achievement	Goals and success, reaching improvements
	Power	Organizing for impact and people outcomes
Small City Climate Urban 2	Affiliation	Relationships and personal values
	Power	Organizing for impact and people outcomes
Rural Climate (Small Town, Farm)	Affiliation	Relationships and personal values
	Personal Causation	Creative and innovative within reality focus

Figure 7-8
Location Climate Predominant Motives

In a large city climate, the predominant motives would be *achievement* and *power*. The *achievement* motive would be present due to the many opportunities people have to advance their position in life. In order to be better at something, you need the opportunities to pursue improvement. Larger cities provide these opportunities due to having more businesses, school systems, higher education opportunities, and a myriad of social and entertainment enterprises. Due to the size of a city and its various opportunities, efforts need to be organized, coordinated, and regulated for the good of all, which fits the *power* motive.

A small city climate also has the need for organization, hence the *power* motive, but also the need to understand and work with relationships highlighting the importance of the *affiliation* motive. There is an implied value structure that makes up the city, and knowing it is important when moving into this Motive Climate.

The rural climate has its basis in the *affiliation* motive. People in this climate are concerned about how they value each other and their relationships. They depend on relationships to keep their area active and somewhat productive. The need for organization is supplanted by being innovative as in the *personal causation* motive. New or novel ideas can find traction since there is little resistance from structured organizing and controlling approaches. For example, building laws and regulations are much fewer in a rural setting, and it is not unusual to find a broad mixture of housing styles, unlike larger cities that have housing neighborhoods that are usually homogeneous and built according to regulations at the time.

When changing or moving from one motive climate to another, consideration should be made about the predominant motives in each of the climates. In Figure 7-9 we can see that there are 6 changes possible, each of which will be briefly reviewed. Some changes are easier than others since they have shared motive.

		To		
		Large City Urban 1 *achievement power*	Small City Urban 2 *affiliation power*	Rural Small Town *affiliation pers cause*
From	Large City Urban 1 *Achi Pow*		1 Shared *power*	2 Shared nothing
	Small City Urban 2 *affil pow*	3 Shared *power*		4 Shared *affiliation*
	Rural Small Town *affil pers cause*	5 Shared nothing	6 Shared *affiliation*	

Figure 7-9
Changing Location Motive Climates

1. Changing from Large City to Small City Climate

You will have to get to know people in their various environments. In one place people may act one way, and another they act differently. Relationships are a function of the how things are organized and controlled. For a large city climate, people are all in it together. But for someone coming from a large city, it is as if people are different depending on their circumstance. How people normally act at work could be quite different from how they act socially. Relationships drive the behavior more so in smaller cities.

2. Changing from Large City to Rural Climate

Relationships are critical, and who you are and what you value defines your role in this climate. No matter the circumstance, you are seen as a particular kind of person. Your relationships define more who you are than what you have accomplished or your social credentials. This can be upsetting since you expect to act according to what you are doing at the time. Also, it may seem like the "wild west" since people think nothing of modifying how they approach things (you may never know when the ice-cream store closes).

3. Changing from Small City to Large City Climate

Everyone seems in a big hurry and has little time for both relationships and consideration of personal values. The environment is well organized, but people do not seem to know each personally. What relationships there are rely often on cliques that you may find hard to join.

4. Changing from Small City to Rural Climate

Everybody seems to know all your business and what you do. The privacy that you may have had is lacking. The routine in this climate often changes because of differing circumstances such as weather, the season of year, and special occasions such as holidays and family celebrations.

5. Changing from Rural to Large City Climate

You would find the big city confining, and giving off the impression that no one really cares about anyone else. The relationships that seemed to occur naturally in a rural environment, must be given special attention in the big city climate. It seems like you almost must decide ahead of time the type of people you would like to associate with by picking the right neighborhood, clubs and church to join, and including the kinds of events to attend (and you would find different crowd at each event).

6. Changing from Rural to Small City Climate

The small city climate seems very confusing at times. There are many rules that seem to be required in order to interact with other people. There are differing expectations depending upon what event or activity is taking place. People seem to be social chameleons who change their spots according to what they are doing.

Change - Retiring from Work

When retiring, whether optional or mandatory, there are several things that need to be considered. The main elements one must consider as one transitions to retirement are financial position, age and health, and family relationships. Personally, speaking as a recently retired person, I have approached retirement as something you have to learn to do. With this in mind, the learning curve will be used to articulate the process of retirement. Transitioning to a mature retirement involves four steps in the learning curve (see Figure 7-10), and with these four steps it is possible to end up being a very satisfied retiree, with a life that is fulfilling and pleasurable. The four steps are 1. Initial Transition, 2. Performance Discovery, 3. New Realization, and 4. Balanced Maturity.

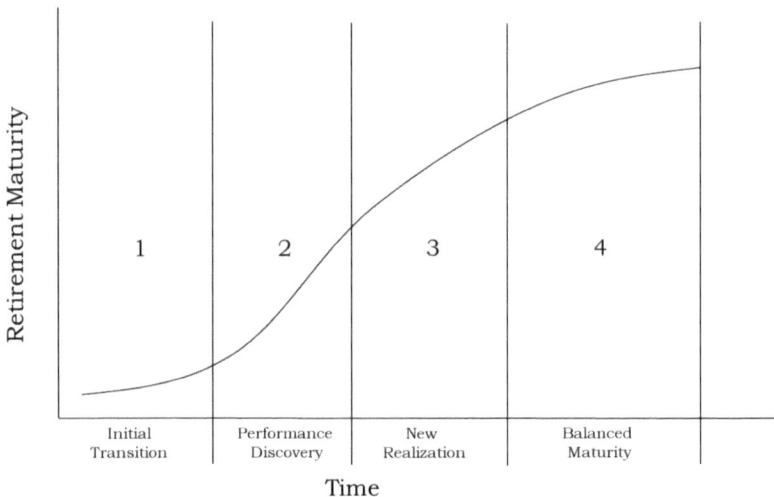

Figure 7-10
Retirement Steps

1. Initial Transition Step

This is perhaps the most important of the four steps. If this step is not executed well, then successful transition through the other steps is in question. What happens in this initial step is the transition from the actual work environment to the retirement environment. To make this transition be as smooth as possible you need to look at the primary motives involved in the work environment, and how they can be matched or accommodated in retirement. The four motives of *achievement, affiliation, power,* and *personal causation* need to be accommodated. This is done by preparing before and at the beginning of retirement to keep the primary motive(s) present in your life.

Achievement Transition Need

An *achievement*-oriented enterprise usually involves setting goals and pursuing these goals so the enterprise and the people in it can be successful. It should also be evident that at retirement if you are used to that *achievement*-oriented way, then it would be best to continue with it. Before you retire, it would be a good idea to set *achievement* goals for retirement. They should take into account what is going to happen immediately after retirement as well as the following years. This could involve what you would do, and when you would do it, such as, taking special trips, visiting family, taking on a part-time job, getting involved in benevolent work, or taking advantage of social and entertainment opportunities. By setting up *achievement* goals the transition between the workplace that has a high *achievement* orientation, and retirement should be smoother.

As an example, when Martha saw retirement was coming, she set aside time to put goals together for what she would do after retirement. The first thing she wanted to do was to buy symphony tickets so that she and her husband could attend the symphony orchestra performances as she had always wanted to do this, but at the last-minute late-night work had always prevented it. The next goal she put down was to volunteer one day a week during Christmas to collect money for those less fortunate. She then set a goal to visit her son's family out of state six times during the year. She also set a goal to have two special nights during the week. The first night she set aside would be for her and her husband to have a date night. The second night was set aside for herself to take up aerobics' classes at the local YMCA. Once Martha retires, she has goals now that she can continue to work on, just as she had goals at her job. Her *achievement* motive is still engaged.

Affiliation Transition Need

When someone retires who has been very close to the people with whom they work, the *affiliation* motive is very important in the transition phase from working to retirement.

When a close friend of mine faced retirement, he found it successful because the *affiliation* that he had at work continued after he retired. The *affiliation* need was served both from the former co-workers, as well as the many friendships he and his wife had made during his years of marriage. His *affiliation* motive was engaged when he met with fellow workers in a local bar between shifts so that they could discuss what had just happened at work during the day shift, and what needed to happen next during the night shift. These fellow workers became close friends with each other along with others in the bar, so that when retirement came those friendships continued. As a result of these other friendships, he took up new sports and hobbies, such as, golf when he retired. No one looked more joyful in retirement than him.

Power Transition Need

If you are engaged in a large enterprise before retirement, then the *power* motive comes into play both when employed and when retired. The *power* motive is mostly about organizing tasks and efforts so that everyone can be successful. When it comes to a business enterprise, this could mean both organizing to surviving in a competitive market, as well as integrating tasks together to function effectively. It is about organizing and controlling the overall environment of the workplace. As in the *power* oriented workplace, retirement transition can be smoothed if there is an element of organizing and controlling activities during this transitional step.

I am reminded of Keven having worked for large enterprises, who at retirement took it upon himself, using social media and emails, to organize all the people he worked with and for to attend individual wine tastings and other get togethers. He took the organizing activities of his workplaces and continued with them at retirement.

Personal Causation Transition Need

When a position you are retiring from requires a great deal of ingenuity, creativity, and sometimes innovation, the *personal causation* motive, a smooth transition to retirement requires these elements. In some cases, people excel in retirement because they are now free to use more creativity and innovation where they may have been hindered somewhat before. A good example of this is former United States president Jimmy Carter and what happened in his life after retiring from the presidency.

Early on in Jimmy Carter's life he was a member of the United States Navy and had graduated from the Naval Academy. He spent several years serving in the Navy until the death of his father at which time he requested a release from duties so he could go back to the family business. The family business was not in good shape, and his father was very forgiving of people and debts, thus, the business suffered significantly. Jimmy Carter took over the peanut business and through his creativity made it a success.

During his presidency his need to be creative and innovative, and less organizing and controlling, oftentimes left him not willing to delegate, resulting in delayed critical decisions that ended up producing negative popular opinion. As a matter of fact, some people believe that Jimmy Carter's presidency was not nearly as effective as his post presidency life. He went on after retirement transitioning to a life of new ventures. "Carter is widely considered a better man than he was a president" noted one popular publication. "Although his presidency received a mixed reception, his peacekeeping and humanitarian efforts since leaving office have made Carter renowned as one of the most successful ex-presidents in American history" as reported in PBS's *American Experience.* He established the Carter Center for promoting and expanding human rights. He received the Nobel Peace Prize for his activities in founding the center. Jimmy Carter conducted peace negotiations, monitored elections, and advanced disease prevention and eradication in developing nations. Carter was a key figure in the nonprofit enterprise Habitat for Humanity. His creativity continued as he authored more than 30 books ranging from political memoirs to poetry. Clearly this is a successful transition to retirement led by a continuing *personal causation* motive presence.

2. Performance Discovery Step

In this step you learn if the ways that you transitioned to retirement have been successful, and you expand your energies to engage in your transitioned motive. It is more of the same but driven by new opportunities that present themselves as exemplified by Jimmy Carter. This is where the retirement transition jumps into high speed and satisfaction grows. However, there comes a point where more of the same is not satisfactory, and slight downturn in motive behaviors occurs initiating Step 3.

3. New Realization Step

Here retirement takes on a new perspective. After having lived through the transitional experiences of Steps 1 and 2, in this step you will find new ways of experiencing what retirement can mean. New motives come into play as differing opportunities present themselves and you take advantage of these. Satisfaction in retirement becomes redefined. Sometimes this means more activities in retirement and sometimes less activities. In some ways we could say Step 3 initiates the wisdom of retirement. One gets the sense that, "I really don't have to be who I have always been, nor do what I have always done."

4. Balanced Maturity Step

In this step retirement satisfaction becomes a balance between efforts and availability of time. What produced satisfaction in earlier steps is no longer considered critical in this step. This can be due to many of the things that you wanted to do which you have already done. That narrows the focus of opportunities that you have, along with the realization that there is a finite number of years to experience life as you would like it. This step of retirement may produce the most satisfaction, since you now have an abundance of experiences to inform you about how you would like to continue your life.

There are many other instances of life changes that we could examine such as marriage, starting a family, death of a loved one, and renewing a spiritual life. Each of these can be examined by the natural motives involved. Insights that can be gained include deciding if and how the change could be made, making the change easier, more pleasant, and how others might be helpful. We have often heard how hard it is to make a change, but after reviewing the changes you have made in your life, you can sometimes see the real value of a change. You should be aware that natural motives analysis reveals that motives themselves can be changed. Your approach to a motive change can involve both training and coaching. Using natural motives is a way to both generate the confidence to make a change and help the process itself. The motives assessments and analyses provided in this book can make a positive difference in your life changes.

Compatibility and Motives

Compatibility between two individuals can be facilitated by knowing each other's predominant motives. A motives analysis using all four motives, both natural and cognitive, provides an overwhelming number of alternatives. To simplify, an example using two Comparative Motive Analysis charts is provided below showing results for two people, Ava and Floyd (see Figure 7-11). Ava's predominant motive is *power* while Floyd's predominant motive is *achievement.* Ava does not understand why Floyd spends so much time trying out new things and setting up new goals for himself and their family. Meanwhile Floyd does not understand why Ava has to have everything controlled and organized. For vacations Ava wants to have them planned and organized so they know exactly when they are going to leave, where they will stop on the way, and when they will arrive at their destination. Floyd would just like to venture out and stop when they feel like stopping, looking at things along the way, and finding creative side-trips as they go. However, they share the natural motive of *personal causation,* although Ava is somewhat unaware that she has the motive. It allows them to share a desire to be creative, but for Ava she is fine with being creative as long as it is somewhat controlled.

Their *affiliation* motive indicates that Eva is not terribly interested in establishing and maintaining relationships with others. She scores low on this natural motive, although she believes she is an average person in this respect. Floyd has a natural inclination for establishing and maintaining relationships, although he is unaware of it. Consequently, they probably have few friends and do not initiate many social get-togethers. Their social engagements usually involve a small set of friends, and they avoid large social gatherings. When they do connect with new people Floyd wonders why they do not seem to do more of it.

Ava and Floyd are incompatible in their predominant motives but share a secondary motive of *personal causation*. They do not make friends easily but are both accept that. They could increase their compatibility by reviewing their motives and realizing what they share and do not share as motives. The outcome could be more enjoyable vacations along with adding new friends as their lives unfold. They also could go beyond just knowing each other's motives by actually learning them. Also, Ava could be trained in *achievement* and Floyd trained in *power*. Results could make them more compatible and share in each other's interests – Floyd would come to enjoy planning as Ava does, and Ava enjoy being more creative and spontaneous matching Floyd's interests.

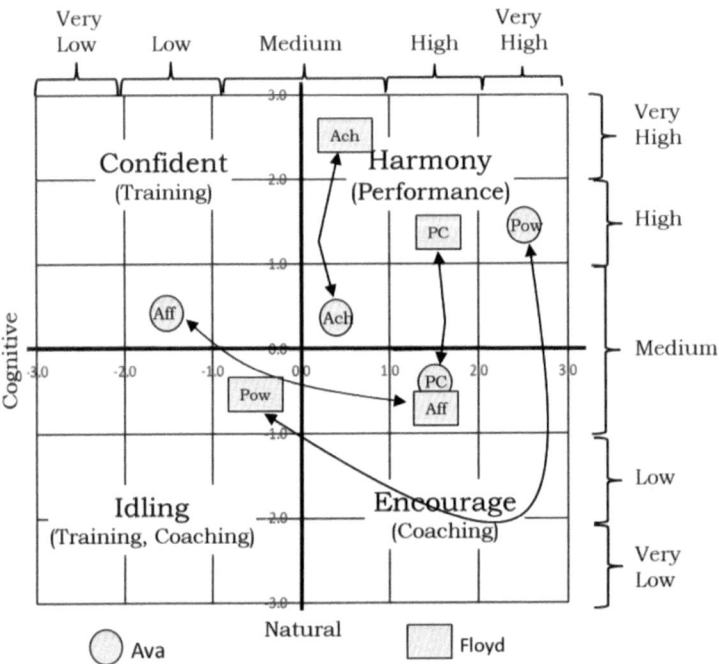

Figure 7-11
Comparative Motive Analysis
(Ava and Floyd Example)

In another example of compatibility, now between Terry and Lora, the following is shown below. Results of a Comparison Motive Analysis of the four motives are provided in the charts in Figure 7-12. Terry's predominant natural motive is *affiliation*, while Lora's predominant natural motive is *power*. There is an incompatibility between the power motives. Terry thinks he has the ability to organize and control circumstances, but he does not have the natural interest to actually do so. For instance, he might say that he wants to organize and plan the remodel of their basement. But since he does not have a natural motive to do it, he procrastinates and plans never seem to develop. While on the other hand, Lora is very strong naturally in *power* but is unaware of it. She does not see why Terry cannot seem to make headway on plans for the remodel. Planning is a natural interest for Lora, but she does not do it because she is unaware it would be a natural interest to her. Terry procrastinates when planning, and Lora would be an active planner if she decided to do it. This could cause division or incompatibility between Terry and Laura. Terry wants to control what needs to be done but lacks the genuine interest to do so, while Lora has the natural interest to control circumstances, but lacks the knowledge that she would be a natural at it.

Lora believes she has a natural *affiliation* motive. That is, she would enjoy meeting and making new friends, while keeping current friends and family active in their social life. But when it comes to planning social events, for which she is naturally suited, she does not seem to do so. Her interest does not lie in being with a lot of people. This frustrates Terry because he has a natural ability to affiliate, and is very interested in keeping connected and making new friends.

Unless they learn to respect their natural interests, there may be an incompatibility that cannot be overcome. Difficulties arise when individuals believe they have interest, as represented by Terry and *power* and Lora with *affiliation*, that they do not have. Conversely, the other person naturally has the interest. One might hear a comment by Terry saying "Why can't Lora be more engaging with their friends and family," and Lora disgusted with Terry comments "He cannot seem to get his act together to get anything done." Results could be that Lora has the opinion that Terry is lazy, and Terry has the opinion that Lora is an uncaring person. Revealing underlying motives can be a first step to alleviate this incompatibility, and put them on a pathway to a more compatible relationship.

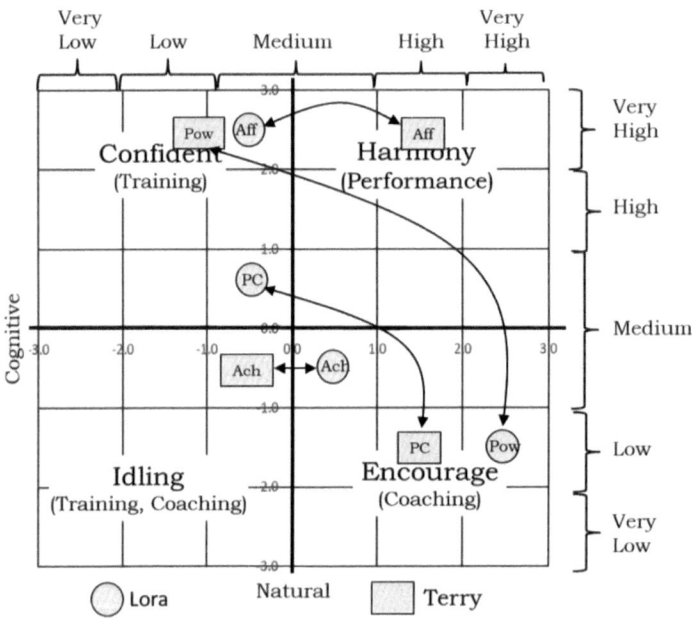

Figure 7-12
Comparative Motive Analysis
(Terry and Lora Example)

Motive analysis can tell us a lot about why people seem to be drawn to the many opportunities that life hands us. They can be used to explain why some jobs seem right and others do not, why some locations suit us and others do not, and even why we are compatible with some people and not others. Motives are the key to understand much of what we do in life.

Motives in Your Life

Motives in Your Life

Appendix 1

Short Motives Assessments with Example

Using this Appendix you can discover in a relatively short time your cognitive and natural motives. Here are the steps:

1. Fill out the short cognitive assessment that follows.
2. Score the cognitive assessment.
   Each of the 4 motives will be scored from very low to very high
3. Using the picture prompts, write stories as directed. This Appendix can be used for quicker scoring rather than the more detailed and standard scoring shown in Appendix 2.
4. Score stories using the information in this Appendix looking to see if a story has one or more of the motives. Each story can be scored once per motive (scores 0-4 per motive.) One story can contain none or even all 4 motives.
5. Analyze the motives using the chart that compares each of the motives against the others, as well as how they score relative to each other for natural versus cognitive motives.

Motives in Your Life

<u>Short Cognitive Motive Questionnaire</u>

Score each of the following 12 items that best fit who you are (range is 0-3)

0 – not fit me; 1 – somewhat fits me; 2 – fits me; 3 – really fits me

_____ 1. I argue with zest for my point of view against others.

_____ 2. I set difficult goals for myself, which I attempt to reach.

_____ 3. I can accomplish almost anything I try.

_____ 4. I enjoy organizing or directing activities of a group - team, club, or committee.

_____ 5. I am in my element when I am with a group of people who enjoy life.

_____ 6. I enjoy relaxation wholeheartedly only when it follows the successful completion of a substantial piece of work.

_____ 7. I become very attached to my friends.

_____ 8. Rules are designed to help and protect everyone.

_____ 9. I enjoy work as much as play.

_____ 10. I feel that I can dominate a social situation.

_____ 11. I go out of my way to be with friends.

_____ 12. In general, I control the activities in my life.

Add the scores for items that are associated with question numbers (range 0 – 9).

Questions 2, 6, 9 _____ Achievement

Questions 5, 7, 11 _____ Affiliation

Questions 1,4,10 _____ Power

Questions 3,8,12 _____ Personal Causation

Cognitive Motives Key

0 – total score – Very Low

1-2 – total score – Low

3-5 – total score – Medium

6-7 – total score – High

8-9 – total score – Very High

Instructions

There are four pictures followed by the 6 general questions:

What is happening?

Who are the people?

What happened before?

What are the people thinking about and feeling?

What do they want?

What will happen next?

These questions are provided on the page that follows each picture, and space is provided on the page so you can write a brief story that comes to mind as you consider the general questions above. Please look at the picture for 15 seconds and then go to the following page and write your brief story. Take no more than 5 minutes for each brief story and do not return to the picture for a second look

Picture 1

Please look at this picture for 15 seconds then turn the page.

Motives in Your Life

Please jot down answers to these questions in a
general story form (no issues with grammar, spelling
etc. need be considered). Take 5 minutes.

What is happening?
Who are the people?
What happened before?
What are the people thinking about and feeling?
What do they want?
What will happen next?

_____

Motives in Your Life

Motives in Your Life

Picture 2

Please look at this picture for 15 seconds then turn
the page.

Motives in Your Life

Please jot down answers to these questions in a general story form (no issues with grammar, spelling etc. need be considered). Take 5 minutes.

What is happening?
Who are the people?
What happened before?
What are the people thinking about and feeling?
What do they want?
What will happen next?

Motives in Your Life

Motives in Your Life

Picture 3

Please look at this picture for 15 seconds then turn the page.

Please jot down answers to these questions in a general story form (no issues with grammar, spelling etc. need be considered). Take 5 minutes.

What is happening?
Who are the people?
What happened before?
What are the people thinking about and feeling?
What do they want?
What will happen next?

Motives in Your Life

Motives in Your Life

Picture 4

Please look at this picture for 15 seconds then turn
the page.

Motives in Your Life

Please jot down answers to these questions in a general story form (no issues with grammar, spelling etc. need be considered). Take 5 minutes.

What is happening?
Who are the people?
What happened before?
What are the people thinking about and feeling?
What do they want?
What will happen next?

_____

Motives in Your Life

Short Natural Motive Assessment (from stories)

Check the story number if the central characteristic is present in the story. Note: more than one characteristic can occur in a single story, but characteristics can only be checked once (max of 4 checks for all stories.)

Story Central Characteristics	Stories				
	1	2	3	4	Sum
Achievement A. Competition with a standard of excellence B. Explicitly stated desire to win (in competitive game) C. Unique accomplishment, as an example, not run of the mill but something that marks the person as a personal success (inventions, artistic creations), or long-term involvement D. Long-term achievement goal as being a success in life (becoming a doctor, lawyer, successful businessman)					

Affiliation					
A. Evidence of a concern in one or more of the characters over establishing, maintaining, or renewing a positive affective relationship with another person. The relationship is most often seen as friendly – seeking some form of friendship. Concern is how one feels about the other or their relationship. Statements of being liked, or accepted, or forgiven could be present. Circumstances could be of acceptance, rejection, separation, or some disruption of the relationship (time, space, other priorities in life).					
B. Evidence from generally accepted affiliative, compassionate activities such as parties, reunions, visits, or relaxed small talk. Others may be friendly, nurturant acts such as consoling, helping, or being concerned about the happiness or well-being of another. However, these activities should not be scored if they are done out of obligation, or a sense of what is culturally required (e.g. a father protecting his daughter).					

Motives in Your Life

Story Central Characteristics	Stories				
	1	2	3	4	Total
Power A. Evidence of someone showing power concern through actions that in themselves express power. They can be present, in the past, planned or even fantasized. Some explicit examples include: a. Giving help, assistance, advice, or support of another (solicited advice is not scored). b. Trying to control other people through regulating their behavior or conditions of their lives, or seeking information that would affect another's life or actions (searching, investigating, checking up on) such as "They are being sent to get information on other shows." c. Trying to influence, persuade, convince, make a point, or argue with another person.					

Power – continued

    d. Trying to impress someone or the world at large. Examples are creative writing, making news or publicity, trying to win an election, or any action that will attract wide-spread attention. "He took her out to make a good impression on her." "He spent most of the day getting ready so he would get a standing ovation."

    e. Strong forceful actions that affect others (e.g., reprimands, attacks, verbal insults, assaults); gaining the upper hand; or taking advantage of another's weakness to impose one's will. "I told her to get off the horse even if she wanted to ride more."

B. Someone does something that aroused strong positive or negative emotions in others. Others may feel pleasure, delight, awe, gratitude, anger, jealousy, or expressions of interest. "She told him how she felt and he began to weep."

Power – continued					
C. Someone is described as having a concern for reputation or position. The affect should be about public position or prestige. Not scored is something that provides internal satisfaction/dissatisfaction of a private goal. "She was thinking about the impression she had made."					

Motives in Your Life

Story Central Characteristics	Stories				
	1	2	3	4	Total
Personal Causation A Look for someone in the story doing something intentionally to produce a change B Person acting as an origin or taking initiative, independently determining his/her own goals, freely choosing an activity with which to pursue the goal(s), and being realistic about his/her abilities and relationships with others and the environment C An individual in the story decides to get something or some state of affairs. This cannot be imposed by another agency D Two major components are goal setting sequence, and responsibility E Instrumental activity taken by the character on his own and not as a response to someone or something else in the story					

Motives in Your Life

Total the number of check items that are associated with the motive (Range 0 – 4).

_____ Achievement

_____ Affiliation

_____ Power

_____ Personal Causation

<u>Natural Motives Key</u>

0 Checks – Very Low

1 Check – Low

2 Checks – Medium

3 Checks – High

4 Checks – Very High

Analyzing Your Motives

Below is a comparison chart for cognitive and natural motives. By making this comparison you can get a sense of the strengths of your motives; both what you think about your motives (cognitive), and what they are naturally. Plotting them on the graph also can give you a overall perspective.

Motives in Your Life

Motive	Achievement (Ach)		Affiliation (Aff)		Power (Pow)		Pers Causation (PC)	
Assessment	Cognitive	Natural	Cognitive	Natural	Cognitive	Natural	Cognitive	Natural
High...Low								

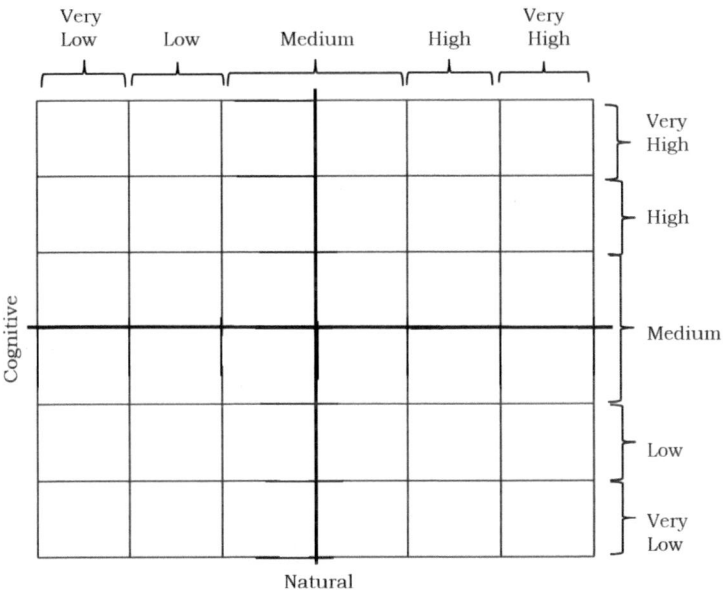

By placing a XXs in the above chart according to your cognitive and natural scores for all 4 motives (X1 for *achievement*; X2 for *affiliation*; X3 for *power*; X4 for *personal causation*) you can get an idea of the relative strengths of your motives. If a natural motive is higher than a cognitive motive, the X would be in the right side of the above chart. If a cognitive motive is higher than a natural motive, the X would be plotted in the upper two quadrants. If a natural motive and its cognitive score are both higher than medium then the X would be in the upper right quadrant. A more detailed example follows.

Example

<u>Short Cognitive Motive Questionnaire</u>
Score each of the following 12 items that best fit who you are (range is 0-3)
0 – not fit me; 1 – somewhat fits me; 2 – fits me; 3 – really fits me

___2__ 1. I argue with zest for my point of view against others.

___2__ 2. I set difficult goals for myself, which I attempt to reach.

___2__ 3. I can accomplish almost anything I try.

___1__ 4. I enjoy organizing or directing activities of a group - team, club, or committee.

___0__ 5. I am in my element when I am with a group of people who enjoy life.

___3__ 6. I enjoy relaxation wholeheartedly only when it follows the successful
completion of a substantial piece of work.

___2__ 7. I become very attached to my friends.

___3__ 8. Rules are designed to help and protect everyone.

___2__ 9. I enjoy work as much as play.

___2__ 10. I feel that I can dominate a social situation.

___1__ 11. I go out of my way to be with friends.

___1__ 12. In general, I control the activities in my life.

Add the scores for items that are associated with question numbers (range 0 – 9).

Questions 2, 6, 9 _____7_____ Achievement – High

Questions 5, 7, 11 _____3_____ Affiliation - Medium

Questions 1,4,10 _____5_____ Power - Medium

Questions 3,8,12 _____6_____ Personal Causation - High

Cognitive Motives Key

   0 – total score – Very Low

1-2 – total score – Low

3-5 – total score – Medium

6-7 – total score – High

8-9 – total score – Very High

Story Central Characteristics	Stories				
	1	2	3	4	Total
Achievement A. Competition with a standard of excellence B. Explicitly stated desire to win (in competitive game) C. Unique accomplishment, as an example, not run of the mill but something that marks the person as a personal success (inventions, artistic creations), or long-term involvement D. Long-term achievement goal as being a success in life (becoming a doctor, lawyer, successful businessman)	X	X	X	X	4

Affiliation					
A. Evidence of a concern in one or more of the characters over establishing, maintaining, or renewing a positive affective relationship with another person. The relationship is most often seen as friendly – seeking some form of friendship. Concern is how one feels about the other or their relationship. Statements of being liked, or accepted, or forgiven could be present. Circumstances could be of acceptance, rejection, separation, or some disruption of the relationship (time, space, other priorities in life).		X		1	
B. Evidence from generally accepted affiliative, compassionate activities such as parties, reunions, visits, or relaxed small talk. Others may be friendly, nurturant acts such as consoling, helping, or being concerned about the happiness or well-being of another. However, these activities should not be scored if they are done out of obligation, or a sense of what is culturally required (e.g. a father protecting his daughter).					

Motives in Your Life

Story Central Characteristics	Stories				
	1	2	3	4	Total
Power A. Evidence of someone showing power concern through actions that in themselves express power. They can be present, in the past, planned or even fantasized. Some explicit examples include: a. Giving help, assistance, advice, or support of another (solicited advice is not scored). b. Trying to control other people through regulating their behavior or conditions of their lives, or seeking information that would affect another's life or actions (searching, investigating, checking up on) such as "They are being sent to get information on other shows." c. Trying to influence, persuade, convince, make a point, or argue with another person.	X	X			2

Power - continued

d. Trying to impress
someone or the world at
large. Examples are creative
writing, making news or
publicity, trying to win an
election, or any action that
will attract wide-spread
attention. "He took her out to
make a good impression on
her." "He spent most of the
day getting ready so he
would get a standing
ovation."
e. Strong forceful actions
that affect others (e.g.,
reprimands, attacks, verbal
insults, assaults); gaining
the upper hand; or taking
advantage of another's
weakness to impose one's
will. "I told her to get off the
horse even if she wanted to
ride more."

B. Someone does something
that aroused strong positive
or negative emotions in
others. Others may feel
pleasure, delight, awe,
gratitude, anger, jealousy, or
expressions of interest. "She
told him how she felt and he
began to weep."

Power - continued C. Someone is described as having a concern for reputation or position. The affect should be about public position or prestige. Not scored is something that provides internal satisfaction/dissatisfaction of a private goal. "She was thinking about the impression she had made."					

Motives in Your Life

Story Central Characteristics	Stories				
	1	2	3	4	Total
Personal Causation					
A Look for someone in the story doing something intentionally to produce a change					
B Person acting as an origin or taking initiative, independently determining his/her own goals, freely choosing an activity with which to pursue the goal(s), and being realistic about his/her abilities and relationships with others and the environment	X	0	X	X	3
C An individual in the story decides to get something or some state of affairs. This cannot be imposed by another agency					
D Two major components are goal setting sequence, and responsibility					
E Instrumental activity taken by the character on his own and not as a response to someone or something else in the story					

Motives in Your Life

Total the number of check items that are associated with the motive (Range 0 – 4).

_____4_____ Achievement -Very High

_____1_____ Affiliation - Low

_____2_____ Power - Medium

_____3_____ Personal Causation - High

Natural Motives Key

0 Checks – Very Low

1 Check – Low

2 Checks – Medium

3 Checks – High

4 Checks – Very High

Motives in Your Life

Motive	Achievement (X1)		Affiliation (X2)		Power (X3)		Pers Causation (X4)	
Assessment	Cognitive	Natural	Cognitive	Natural	Cognitive	Natural	Cognitive	Natural
Scores	**High**	**Very High**	**Medium**	**Low**	**Medium**	**Medium**	**Medium**	**High**

Motives in Your Life

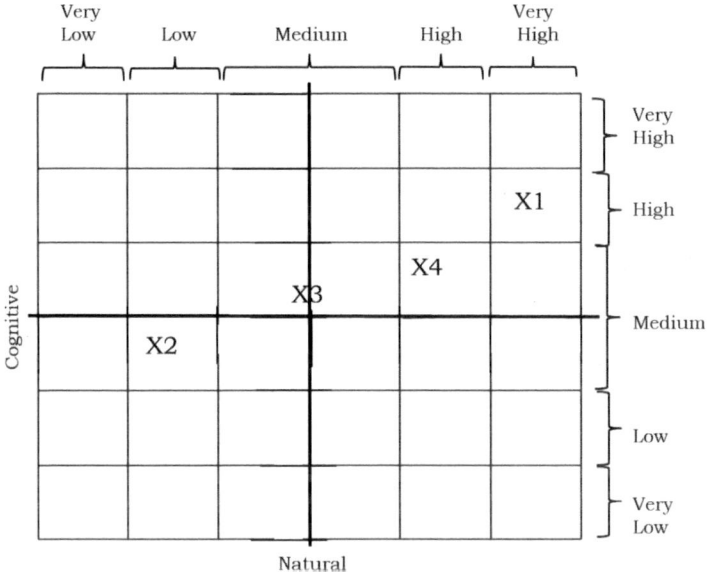

This person is naturally higher in *achievement* (X1) and *personal causation* (X4) than they know (cognitive). They should be encouraged to engaged more in setting goals, and personal creativity. Their low natural and cognitive scores in *affiliation* (X2) may seem okay to them since they see themselves (cognitive) as not really a people person, and are not naturally drawn into situations that require a concern for relationships.

After you have plotted your scores, and with an understanding of these motives, you may come to realize a more fulfilling life approach. (Note: Natural motive scores for each motive can increase with appropriate deep training. Cognitive scores for each motive can increase with counseling to become more aware of current activities that are supported by that motive.)

243

Motives in Your Life

Appendix 2

Motive Training

_____

Motives in Your Life

Elements of Life Assessment

This element in your life brings you what level of satisfaction	None	Somewhat	Acceptable	Very Good	Excellent
1 Friends Being with, making new friends	1	2	3	4	5
2 Future Thing about, looking forward to	1	2	3	4	5
3 Entertainment Enjoying oneself	1	2	3	4	5
4 Work Accomplishing, solving problems	1	2	3	4	5
5 Neighbors Visiting, interacting with	1	2	3	4	5
6 Planning Making plans	1	2	3	4	5
7 Residence Remodeling, maintaining	1	2	3	4	5

Elements of Life Assessment	1	2	3	4	5
8 Spouse/Significant other Spending time, interacting	1	2	3	4	5
9 Politics Discussing, evaluating	1	2	3	4	5
10 Riskiness Overcoming odds	1	2	3	4	5
11 Spiritual Advocating, control by	1	2	3	4	5
12 Hobbies Special interests, for fun	1	2	3	4	5
13 Budget Establishing, maintaining	1	2	3	4	5
14 Food Enjoying favorites	1	2	3	4	5
15 Family Sharing lives, interacting	1	2	3	4	5
16 Travel/new sites Going interesting places	1	2	3	4	5
17 Benevolence For good of others	1	2	3	4	5

To train oneself in a motive means to engage in behavior that reinforces the motive. The above assessment provides elements that could be used to increase that motive.

To improve the *achievement* motive, engage more in these activities:
2 Future, 4 Work, 6 Planning, 7 Residence, 13 Budget

To improve the *affiliation* motive, engage more in these activities:
1 Friends, 5 Neighbors, 8 Spouse, 15 Family, 17 Benevolence

To improve the *power* motive, engage more in these activities:
9 Politics, 10 Riskiness, 11 Spiritual, 13 Budget, 17 Benevolence

To improve the *personal causation* motive, engage more in these activities:
3 Entertainment, 7 Residence, 12 Hobbies, 14 Food, 16 Travel/New Sites

---

(Note: Items 7, 13, and 17 are scored in more than one motive)

Formal Motive Training

Each of the four motives, *achievement, affiliation, power,* and *personal causation* can be increased through formal training. Training for each of these motives has been conducted in a classroom setting requiring the participants to be open to learning. There have been before-and-after motive measures in each of these training experiences which demonstrate their effectiveness. While the circumstances of the training are different these instances show the malleability of motives.

Each training experience involved learning the motive along with activities that provided personal experiences of it. Several elements are used as an overall model for each motive training session. These elements are:

6. Know the motive through its definition and descriptions (knowledge)
7. Be able to recognize and score the motive in stories written by others (recognition)
8. Work through exercises that target the motive usage (personal experience)
9. Testimonial of people with a high degree of the motive (encouragement)
10. Personal description of what to do to increase the motive (commitment)

Mentors and coaches can help suggest training and provide a level of inspiration to keep commitments (also, see Chapter 2.)

Motives in Your Life

Index

"

"Sully" Sullenberger, 93

A

achievement, ii, 2, 10, 11, 12, 15, 16, 19, 20, 25, 29, 31, 34, 40,
   41, 48, 49, 52, 57, 58, 59, 63, 67, 70, 71, 107, 109, 110, 111, 113,
   114, 115, 119, 128, 129, 130, 131, 132, 133, 134, 137, 138, 139,
   140, 141, 142, 148, 149, 151, 152, 153, 154, 155, 157, 159, 161,
   162, 165, 166, 168, 173, 176, 177, 179, 181, 185, 187, 190, 191,
   196, 197, 222, 231, 234, 243, 248
affiliation, ii, 2, 11, 16, 17, 19, 20, 21, 25, 29, 31, 33, 35, 40, 41,
   48, 57, 58, 59, 63, 66, 68, 70, 99, 105, 107, 109, 111, 113, 114,
   115, 119, 128, 129, 130, 131, 132, 133, 134, 137, 138, 139, 140,
   141, 142, 148, 149, 151, 152, 154, 155, 156, 157, 158, 159,
   161,162, 165, 166, 167, 168, 173, 176, 181, 186, 187, 190, 192,
   197, 198, 199, 231, 243, 248
Alignment, 8
Ambassador, 19, 63, 64, 65, 68, 71, 72, 84, 95, 96
Anchor Point, 128, 129
Arnold Palmer, 47, 48, 49
Assessment, 34, 36, 175, 222
assessments, 20, 25, 32, 34, 44, 45, 46, 59, 139, 173, 180, 196
automobile racing, 154
Availability Heuristic, 128, 132

B

Behavior Potential, 2, 7, 8, 9, 10, 12, 13, 14, 24, 61, 121, 166,
   168
Behavioral Economics, 121, 126, 127, 141, 148, 150
Bias, 128, 129, 133, 134, 136, 137, 138, 139
biases, 127, 128, 129, 131, 141, 148
Biases, 128

C

Candid, 151, 152, 153, 159, 161, 164

capacity, 9, 10, 144, 166

career, 8, 11, 12, 13, 20, 32, 52, 53, 66, 101, 102, 103, 104, 105, 106, 107, 109, 110, 111, 115, 116, 119, 131, 161, 179, 180

Career, 107, 109

Careers, 20, 101, 107, 109, 179

Changing Jobs, 181

Changing Locations, 184

character, iii, iv, 10, 19, 44, 56, 227, 240

Chick-fil-A, 70, 72

Choices, 121, 127, 148

Christian-oriented, 156

Closure, 150

Cognitive Motive Questionnaire, 204, 232

cognitive motives, ii, 171, 180, 203

comparative Motive Analysis (CMA) Chart, 172

Comparative Motive Analysis Chart, 172, 176, 180

Compatibility, 196

Controlling, 114, 119, 152, 153, 161

Controlling syndrome, 114, 119

Coordinating syndrome, 109

COVID-19, 94

Creative, 152, 153, 155, 185

cultural, 33, 34, 67, 71

culture, 61, 69, 70, 71, 72, 73, 96, 97, 99, 150, 181

D

Directing syndrome, 111

DiSC, 32

Doer, 20, 22, 32, 63, 64, 65, 177

dominant response, 164, 165

Dwight D. Eisenhower, 66, 72

E

Eleanor Roosevelt, 20, 22, 48, 49, 171

elementary teacher, 157

Emotional, 53

Endowment, 129, 139

equity, 166, 167, 168, 169

Event Organizers, 163

F

familial, 69, 70, 71, 73
Framing, 128, 133, 136
Fraternities, 161

G

Goal, 12
Group Identity, 149, 152
Group motive, 149, 152, 163
groups, iii, iv, 7, 8, 16, 20, 29, 149, 153, 154, 155, 156, 157, 158, 159, 162, 163, 164, 166, 168
Groups, 20, 150, 152, 154, 156, 158, 160, 162, 163, 166

H

Hell's Angels, 154
heuristics, 127, 128, 129, 131, 134, 141, 148
Heuristics, 128, 129, 130, 135
Hobbies, 52, 248

I

Immediacy, 152, 154
Indeterminant Leadership Role (L4), 94
Influencer, 19, 63, 64, 65, 66, 71, 72, 83, 84, 95, 96, 99
Influential, 152, 153, 156
Initiating syndrome, 113, 119
Initiator, 20, 22, 32, 63, 64, 65, 113
Innovator, 63, 64, 65, 67, 71, 96
Insistent, 152, 153

J

John F. Kennedy, 158
John Grisham, 52
John Madden, 160

K

Kahneman, 127
K-Mart, 90

L

leadership, ii, 2, 16, 34, 61, 62, 63, 68, 69, 70, 71, 72, 73, 74, 75, 76, 78, 79, 80, 81, 83, 85, 86, 87, 93, 94, 95, 96, 97, 99, 115, 179
Leadership, 20, 61, 62, 63, 64, 65, 68, 69, 72, 73, 75, 76, 77, 78, 82, 84, 86, 90, 91, 92, 94, 96, 98
leadership philosophy, 68, 73, 75, 79, 80, 81, 97
Leadership Roles, 84, 96
Leading syndrome, 115
Learning, 46, 47, 51, 53, 54
Leonard, George, 55

M

Management/Operations Leadership Role (L3), 92
Margaret Thatcher, 20, 22, 66, 72
Martin Luther King's assassination, 157
Master, 54
Mastery, 54, 55
MBTI, 32, 45
Moral, 152, 153, 157, 164
Motive Climate, 184, 185, 186
Motive Counseling, 179
Motive Training, 245, 247, 248
motives, ii, iii, v, 1, 8, 9, 10, 11, 12, 13, 14, 15, 16, 18, 19, 20, 22, 24, 25, 26, 27, 29, 31, 32, 33, 34, 36, 41, 45, 46, 47, 48, 52, 56, 57, 59, 61, 62, 63, 66, 67, 68, 70, 72, 83, 96, 99, 105, 106, 107, 115, 119, 121, 126, 129, 130, 131, 137, 138, 139, 141,144, 148, 149, 151, 152, 153, 154, 155, 156, 159, 161, 162, 163, 164, 171, 172, 173, 177, 179, 180, 181, 182, 184, 185, 186, 190, 195, 196, 197, 198, 199, 203, 229, 231, 243, 248
Motives, ii, iii, 1, 7, 11, 14, 15, 16, 19, 22, 25, 26, 27, 28, 29, 32, 34, 41, 44, 45, 46, 49, 50, 51, 53, 57, 59, 61, 62, 63, 64, 84, 96, 101, 121, 127, 128, 129, 137, 141, 148, 153, 159, 160, 171, 181, 182, 185, 196, 200, 203, 205, 228, 229, 233, 241
Mover, 63, 64, 65, 66, 67, 71, 72, 84, 95, 96, 179
Multi-Tasking, 128, 137
Mutuality syndrome, 110

N

natural motives, ii, iii, v, 8, 10, 11, 12, 13, 14, 20, 24, 33, 49, 105, 106, 119, 171, 179, 196

O

opportunities, v, 2, 7, 9, 10, 12, 13, 14, 16, 18, 19, 24, 49, 50, 51, 54, 63, 86, 97, 111, 119, 166, 168, 173, 179, 180, 185, 191, 194, 195, 200

ordered, 69, 70, 71, 73, 91

organizational culture, 69, 71, 97, 99

Overcomer, 19, 20, 22, 32, 63, 64, 65, 177

P

People/Human Leadership Role (L2), 91

Performative, 152, 153, 162

personal causation, ii, 2, 11, 16, 18, 19, 20, 21, 26, 29, 31, 33, 48, 49, 52, 57, 59, 63, 67, 68, 70, 107, 110, 111, 113, 114, 115, 119, 128, 129, 130, 132, 133, 134, 137, 139, 142, 143, 148, 152, 153, 154, 155, 157, 159, 161, 162, 163, 166, 168, 173, 176, 177, 182, 186, 190, 193, 194, 196, 197, 231, 243, 248

personality, ii, 19, 29, 31, 45, 63, 67, 89, 91, 92, 177

Persuader, 19, 20, 22, 32, 63, 64, 65

Plateaus, 55

power, ii, 2, 11, 16, 17, 19, 20, 21, 25, 26, 29, 31, 33, 42, 49, 57, 58, 59, 61, 63, 66, 67, 70, 75, 78, 99, 107, 109, 111, 113, 114, 115, 119, 128, 129, 130, 131, 132, 135, 137, 139, 141, 142, 148, 149, 152, 154, 155, 156, 157, 159, 161, 162, 163, 166, 167, 173, 176, 177, 179, 181, 185, 186, 187, 190, 192, 196, 197, 198, 199, 224, 231, 237, 248

prejudices, 159

preseason sports camp/tryout, 154

professional, iv, iii, 47, 62, 89, 93, 102, 105, 123, 154, 156, 160, 164

R

Representativeness Heuristic, 128, 131

Retirement Steps, 190

Retiring from Work, 189

S

Saint Teresa, 68

self-actualization, 15

self-fulfilled, 8

Sensitive, 65, 152, 153, 156

Shackleton, 79, 80
Shirking, 165
Social facilitation, 164
social statuses, 69
Soviet Union, 66, 158
sports teams, 160
Steve Jobs, 65, 67, 72
stories, i, 33, 41, 52, 57, 58, 59, 123, 203, 222, 249
Strategic/Executive (L1) role, 87, 91
surgical team, 162
syndromes, iii, 19, 20, 22, 24, 25, 29, 31, 32, 62, 63, 69, 71, 83,
    96, 97, 99, 107, 116, 141, 142, 144, 148, 149, 152, 153, 163, 164,
    165
Syndromes, 2, 19, 22, 29, 32, 64, 65, 72, 84, 96, 98, 107, 108,
    149, 152, 153, 177, 178

T

Tactful, 82, 152, 153, 161
TAT, iii, iv, v, 33, 44
team, 13, 58, 111, 112, 114, 154, 160, 161, 163, 204, 232
temperaments, 29, 30
The Knowing-Living Gap, 105
theatrical troupe, 162
Thematic Apperception Test, iii, 33, 44
Thinking Speed, 128, 138
Tiger Woods, 47, 48
training, iii, 34, 44, 53, 57, 58, 59, 68, 87, 93, 106, 120, 151, 152,
    173, 179, 182, 196, 243, 248, 249
traits, 27, 29, 30, 31, 87, 89
Tversky, 127

V

Vision, 55

Motives in Your Life